Christy Lane's
Complete Book
of
ing

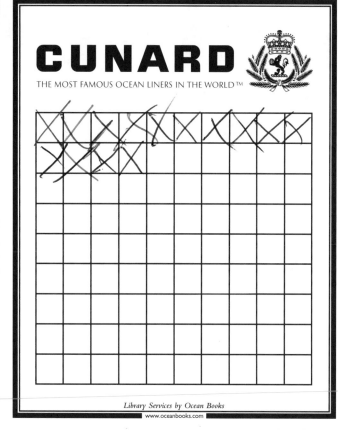

Human Kinetics

Library of Congress Cataloging-in-Publication Data

Lane, Christy.
   [Complete book of line dancing]
   Christy Lane's complete book of line dancing / Christy Lane.--2nd ed.
     p. cm.
   ISBN 0-7360-0067-4
   1. Line dancing. I. Title.
  GV1768.L35   2000
  793.3--dc21   99-048366

ISBN-10: 0-7360-0067-4
ISBN-13: 978-0-7360-0067-3

Acquisitions Editor: Judy Patterson Wright, PhD
Managing Editor: Leigh LaHood
Copyeditor: Fred Smith
Proofreader: Joanna Hatzopoulos
Graphic Designer: Nancy Rasmus
Graphic Artist: Sandra Meier
Cover Designer: Jack W. Davis
Photographer (cover and interior): Pete Moroz
Illustrator: Tom Roberts
Printer: United Graphics

Human Kinetics books are available at special discounts for bulk purchase. Special editions or book excerpts can also be created to specification. For details, contact the Special Sales Manager at Human Kinetics.

Printed in the United States of America

10   9   8   7

Human Kinetics
Web site: www.HumanKinetics.com

United States: Human Kinetics
P.O. Box 5076, Champaign, IL 61825-5076
800-747-4457
e-mail: humank@hkusa.com

Canada: Human Kinetics
475 Devonshire Road Unit 100, Windsor, ON N8Y 2L5
800-465-7301 (in Canada only)
e-mail: info@hkcanada.com

Europe: Human Kinetics
107 Bradford Road, Stanningley, Leeds LS28 6AT, United Kingdom
+44 (0) 113 255 5665
e-mail: hk@hkeurope.com

Australia: Human Kinetics
57A Price Avenue, Lower Mitcham, South Australia 5062
08 8372 0999
e-mail: info@hkaustralia.com

New Zealand: Human Kinetics
Division of Sports Distributors NZ Ltd., P.O. Box 300 226 Albany, North Shore City, Auckland
0064 9 448 1207
e-mail: info@humankinetics.co.nz

Contents

Acknowledgments   vi
Welcome to Line Dancing!   vii

Chapter 1   Would You Like to Dance?   1

What's All This Ruckus About Line Dancing?   2   Seven Steps to Success   3

Chapter 2   Know Your Lingo   9

How to Read a Foot Map   10   Line Dancing Terminology   12

Chapter 3   Heel, Toe, Heel, Toe—Here We Go!   19

Beginning Line Dances   **20**   Coyote   42

Cowboy Motion   21   Down and Dirty   44

Freeze   23   Louie   46

Cowboy Boogie   25   Slappin' Leather   49

Electric Slide I   27   One Step Forward, Two Steps Back   52

Bus Stop   29   Electric Slide II   54

Cowgirl's Twist   31   Flying Eight   56

Double Dutch Bus   34   Reggae Cowboy   58

Smooth   36   Tennessee Twister   60

Chattahoochee   38   Cowboy Macarena   62

Cowboy Hustle   40   Hitchhiker   62

Chapter 4   A Little Harder, But a Lot More Fun!   63

Intermediate Line Dances   **64**   Ghostbusters   77

Copperhead Road   65   Hooked on Country   79

Power Jam   67   Night Fever   81

Honky Tonk Stomp   69   Funky Cowboy I   84

Southside Shuffle   71   Tush Push   86

Wild Wild West I   73   Country Strut   89

Amos Moses   75   Outlaw Waltz   92

Six Step 95
Tumbleweed 98
Cowboy Stomp 100
Boot Scoot Boogie I 102
Black Velvet (Ski Bumpus) 104
Elvira 107
Honky Tonk Attitude 110
Watermelon Crawl 113
Thunderfoot 116

Rock Around the Clock 119
Dance Ranch Romp 122
Alley Cat 125
The Redneck 129
Wild Wild West II 133
Livin' La Vida Loca 137
The Gilley 143
Waltz Across Texas 145
Funky Cowboy II 149

Chapter 5 When You Really Get Good . . . 153

Advanced Line Dances 154
  Boot Scoot Boogie II 155
  Walkin' Wazi 158
  Cowboy Cha-Cha 161
  Romeo 163

Achy Breaky 166
LeDoux Shuffle 169
Hip-Hop 174
CHES 180

Chapter 6 Share the Fun With Others! 181

Partner-Pattern Dances 182
  Ten-Step 183
  Cotton-Eyed Joe 184

Barn Dance Mixer 185
Traveling Cha-Cha 186

Chapter 7 Developing Technique and Style 187

Technique 188
Style 188

Variations 189
Attitude 190

Chapter 8 For Teachers Only 191

Facility 192
Equipment 193
Music 194
Attire 195

Class Format 195
Teaching in the Schools 198
Additional Suggestions 198

Acknowledgments

I would like to thank all the dance instructors, dancers, disc jockeys, physical educators, and music teachers around the country who have taken the time to share with me their dances and experiences. I wish there were room to list all of you because you are so significant to the development of this book.

I am very grateful for the guidance and inspiration of my friends: Hillbilly Rick, whose gift of teaching has influenced and delighted thousands of dancers around the world; Dennis Kellams for his patience and dedication to quality teaching; Dawn Snyder for her sincere dedication to research; and Dr. Jerry Krause for his belief in the benefits of dance and his assistance in the video that complements this book. To Erik Gandolfi, Denise Womach, Sandy Mueller, Pete Moroz, Lorna Hamilton, and Mary Yager, thank you always for your unconditional support on this project and for your friendship. To Bonnie Mohnsen and Jennifer Gorecki, thank you for your assistance on the teacher's section of this book and bravo for your dedication to the teaching profession. To Nancy Kellogg, Susan Padilla, Charlie Griswold, Kristen Griswold, Robin Bates, Sue Cheers, and Linnea Erickson, your assistance was appreciated.

I would also like to thank the models who appear in the photos: Lorna Hamilton, Jason Maxwell, Kelly Lane, April Wolfe, Dennis Kellams, Mary Yager, Don Yager, Mathew Bergam, Amy Harwood, Nichole Bergam, Kristopher Harwood, Brian Egger, Steve Kramer, Lelania Maxwell, Shawn Maxwell, Craig Marquardt, Ann Koegen, Jeneed D. Barratt, Mary Gunasakara, Ran Jan Gunasakara, Sandra C. Mueller, and Debbi Freedman.

Oh yes, and thank you, Megan Paternoster, for your enthusiastic contribution to this book.

Welcome to Line Dancing!

Well, well, here we are again. I just finished teaching line dance at another exciting event, and, again, my heart feels warm as I reminisce over the evening's activities. I wish I could tell you that I pulled up on my horse with my dusty covered chaps, but I didn't. I flew in on another 747 and was wearing the hottest rhinestone outfit I could find. I wish I could tell you that I taught in the red barn, hay and all, but I didn't. I taught in a high-tech convention center complete with big screens and top-of-the-line multimedia. I wish I could tell you that I learned all the dances from my good ol' cowboy friends, but I didn't. I will confess to you that I went to my computer and searched the Internet as part of my research, enabling me to talk to hundreds of dancers around the world.

Welcome to line dancing in the new millennium! Here it is five years after the first edition of this line dance book. Yes, a lot has changed in line dancing, especially in the last decade. But one thing has stayed the same. Again, an empty room was filled with laughter, fun, good music, and high energy as people of all ages and abilities came together. Over and over I have seen dance become a tremendous outlet—physically, mentally, emotionally, socially, and spiritually—a marvelous way to experience life. And now, again, I have the opportunity to share dance with you in this book—to inform, motivate, and provide you with a great personal reference guide for line dancing. I feel confident that this book will help you develop a working knowledge and appreciation for this wonderful activity.

Line dancing has grown tremendously in popularity. Why? It's fun, energetic, and you don't need a partner. There are thousands of line dances, and people are creating new dances everyday. Today you can just jump onto the dance floor and choose the variations you like, because they are *all* right! The dances you will learn in this revised edition are either the "classic" or the most popular dances, at the time this book was written, based on a national survey. Again you may see variations of these dances in your area, but I guarantee that if you know the dances in this book you will be able to conquer any of those variations without any problems!

Chapter 1 is especially for beginners. It includes suggestions that are both fun and practical to eliminate the fear of the dance floor and get you up and moving. Floor etiquette is defined as well as proper dance alignment. You are going to learn some new things regarding music and line dance history and its place as a dance form among the other dance disciplines. Chapter 2 will get you ready to hit the dance floor by introducing you to updated terminology and teaching you how to read a "foot map."

Chapter 3 illustrates the beginning dances, including the number of steps, how many directions the dance faces, illustrated footwork, written steps, and music suggestions. You will notice that some dances were created to fit just one song but some can be performed to numerous songs. Chapter 4 discusses the intermediate dances, and then chapter 5 describes the most advanced dances. All the dances within each chapter are arranged in a suggested learning order. There are 64 dances—all with complete choreography. Many are danced to popular country, rock, and techno music, but there are also elegant waltzes and stylish cha-chas.

The remaining three chapters of the book offer both variety and challenge. Chapter 6 includes partner-pattern dancing, which is line dancing with a partner. Chapter 7 focuses on tips for dancers, highlighting style, confidence, and enjoyment. If you are a line dance instructor or interested in becoming one, chapter 8 includes useful information about equipment, music sources, class format, and more.

So as I look out of this airplane window once more to view another beautiful sunset, I think how lucky I am to be given the good fortune to share this exciting dance form with so many people. I hope you enjoy your experience in this wonderful world of dance.

As Brooks and Dunn, the famous country duo, put it so nicely, "Get down, turn around, go to town." It's time to put on your dancing shoes, grab a partner, and "boot scoot and boogie!"

Would You Like to Dance?

What a great time to be alive! We are in the middle of one of the biggest dance crazes ever—as big as the Jitterbug was in the 1950s and the Twist in the '60s. Just think, you could have been born in another era and never had the opportunity to learn line dancing. So congratulations for being alive now—because you are about to make history!

First, let me introduce myself. I am your personal line dance instructor, the one crazy enough to create all the little feet you are about to see. And what about you? You must be either a beginning dancer embarking on an exciting adventure into the world of dance or an experienced line dancer in search of current information. If you are experienced, feel free to go right to chapter 2. If you are my Rookie of the Year, not even sure if this is where your dreams will come true, hang on and continue reading because I have some news for you! If you're looking for suggestions to keep you inspired as you work your way through the dances, stick with me. I have some pointers coming up in the next few pages. But first, I want to tell you a little about the history of line dancing and explain why it's so popular today.

What's All This Ruckus About Line Dancing?

Line dancing is, like all other dance forms, a reflection of history and culture. Dance itself has been a form of communication and self-expression since prehistoric times. People have enjoyed dance not only as an art form but also as a way to feel good physically, to be stimulated mentally, to develop self-esteem, and to meet people. For some, dance is even part of the path to spiritual enlightenment.

Line dancing involves people standing in lines and performing dance movements together. It consists of patterned foot movements that are usually performed to a number of counts per sequence, and then the sequence is repeated. The dances are done one-wall, two-wall, or four-wall. After performing the sequence pattern once, you will end facing a different direction (or wall) before repeating the sequence. Sound confusing? Don't be alarmed. Just repeat the same sequence facing the new direction. If you only face two walls during the repeated sequences, you are performing a two-wall dance. If your sequence faces four walls, you are performing a four-wall dance. There are, of course, one-wall dances that continuously repeat the sequence facing toward the front. (Isn't that nice?)

If you were to ask 10 people with some knowledge of dance when line dancing began, you'd probably get 10 different answers. A popular opinion about line dancing is that it is a tradition, not a fad. Some believe this style of dancing has strong ties to folk dancing. In the 1800s, European immigrants traveled west to North America, bringing with them a wealth of culture, including such native dances as the polka and waltz, whose movements joined and evolved into what was called round and square dancing. Many believe that this style of dancing introduced the terms and steps used in country line dancing today. Some people feel it was the cowboys on the western frontier, from the 1860s to the 1890s, that took these more traditional dance moves and assimilated them into a country-western style. Others believe that the settlers of the western states, such as Texas and Oklahoma, should be credited with the simple footwork and the country flair that reflects the culture of their time.

In the early 1900s, schools began to include folk dancing in their physical education programs. Many believe that American servicemen returning home from war influenced the spread of line dancing after being introduced to traditional European folk dances. As large numbers of youth learned country-western dance, its popularity grew in leisure and social activities.

Then there are the patrons of the 1970s who believe that the real popularity of line dancing evolved from the disco era. The steady dance beat of the rhythmic music and the influence of television shows such as *Soul Train* and movies such as *Saturday Night Fever* (starring actor and dancer John Travolta and released in 1978) caused a dance sensation. Line dances were performed to disco-style music.

As the lines between pop and country blurred, John Travolta created a stir again in 1980 with the movie *Urban Cowboy*, which spurred a renewed interest in country culture and a new wave of western fashion, music, and dance. When country music started its rapid ascent in popularity in the mid 1980s, a profusion of bright, talented singers and songwriters burst onto the music charts, giving country music a shot in the arm. Along with the music came the dancing. And with the media behind it, country influence began to sweep through grassroots America.

In 1993, line dancing rose to the forefront when savvy marketers packaged the country-western hit song "Achy Breaky Heart" by Billy Ray Cyrus with a new line dance that swept the country. Many say that "Achy Breaky Heart" was a major turning point in the popularity of line dance.

We do know that the line dance craze of the 1990s demonstrated staying power. Line dancing began incorporating many musical styles besides country, including pop, rock, jazz, disco, Latin, and even Big Band music! Country music began to appear on the pop charts, and line dancing began to cross boundaries of income, race, age, and gender. Singles, as well as families, see line dancing as a healthy social outlet. Numerous opportunities exist for recreational dancing at dance clubs, convention socials, wedding receptions, school-sponsored dances, studio recitals, and dance competitions. Now line dancing is considered an art form of its own, with its own terminology and standardized steps. A social and economic culture has evolved out of country-western line dance events, competitions, trade magazines, and television shows. The popularity of this widely accepted dance form also has grown extensively in other countries.

So why is there such a big attraction to line dancing today? For country dancers, part of the appeal seems to stem from the growing interest in the country way of life. Many people are attracted to the simplicity of the American frontier past and the rugged individualism and close family ties that it represents. Line dancing, in all its different styles, offers several attractions. It is easier than other fad dances and it does not require a partner. It attracts families, singles, and seniors, helping this art form to combine opportunities for individualism with community camaraderie. And it provides an enjoyable way to achieve both mental and physical exercise.

Actually, when you sit back and think about how line dancing is performed, with everyone doing the same movement at the same time, it could have descended from African or Native American dancing. Although the origin may not be clear, one thing is—line dancing is here to stay!

Seven Steps to Success

The best thing about line dancing is that you can't lose! Because line dancing does not require a partner, you do not have to cringe in anticipation of that scary question, "Do you wanna dance?" That's right, no more! When you hear the music, hit the floor. (No, not literally; I mean get on the dance floor and start moving.) It doesn't matter what your age or ability level is because everybody dances with everybody else. Line dancing is performed with a group of people moving in unison to music (most of the time in straight lines, facing the same direction) while having a blast! To get the most out of line dancing, take the following seven steps.

Think Positively

Because of your desire to get out there on the dance floor and look good soon, there's not enough time to tell you throughout the book how great, wonderful, beautiful, individual, and expressive you are. So it's up to you. Do it now. What are you thinking of at this very moment? Are you doubting yourself? If you're planning on going through all that negative stuff, hurry up, I'm waiting. We have things to do, mountains to climb, bridges to cross, and line dancing to learn. You can wait until you're 100 years old to dance; but honestly, I don't have that kind of time and, besides, if you start now, just think how good you'll be at 100! Okay, take a deep breath and then breathe out that negativity—right now. This is the age of the body–mind connection. So, let's adopt the right attitude. You will be 100-percent more effective if you think positively. This is the time to tell your body, "Fred Astaire, here I come!"

Start at the Beginning

I know, some people are born dancers. But don't be intimidated by them. When you look at the dance floor, where do your eyes usually go? To the more advanced (skilled) dancers, the ones you think are naturals. However, most of them started at the beginning, the same way you did—and they practiced, practiced, and practiced some more. That's the key. Of course, there really are "born dancers" out there, but not very many. If you really look around the next time you go out, you will find people falling, tripping, and stepping on toes. Nine times out of ten, they will be laughing! You have to have a good sense of humor whenever you try anything for the first time. So come on, relax and smile. You have to start somewhere. Fortunately, you picked a dance form that is easy to learn. (Thank heavens we do not have to spin on our heads!) Good, you are halfway there.

Go in the Right Direction

Compared to driving the freeways at rush hour, line dancing is a piece of cake! You're bound to bump into someone. If that should happen, smile, be courteous, and just continue dancing. (Besides, stepping on a foot is an interesting way to meet someone new.) Just as the freeway belongs to everyone, so does the dance floor. Of course, it always helps to know which direction to go, and that's where floor etiquette comes into the picture (see figure 1.1). Line dancing is usually done in the middle of the dance floor in an imaginary rectangular space with everyone facing the same direction, unless the dance club or hostess designates another location. Line dancers form several small lines rather than one extended line so as not to block the traveling dancers. This tiny bit of knowledge will keep you from colliding with people. Take note that all the partner dancers move counterclockwise around the dance floor in what is called the "line of dance." Ahhh, so that's it! Now that you know how to "drive" the dancing "freeway," shorten up those steps. This will make you more agile and mobile. Line dancing participants start on the same foot and move in the same direction (thank goodness). So there's nothing to worry about. When everyone goes right, you go right!

Stand Tall

No, this is not your mother speaking. Proper alignment allows you to use your muscles most efficiently and with the least amount of tension. Besides all that, you look better. Do me a favor: stand against a wall. Put your heels against the wall and pull your shoulders back so that your body is in alignment. Try pressing the small of your back into the wall as you lift your stomach and rib cage up and in. Are you breathing? You can think clearer and move faster if you breathe. (Besides that, you won't pass out.)

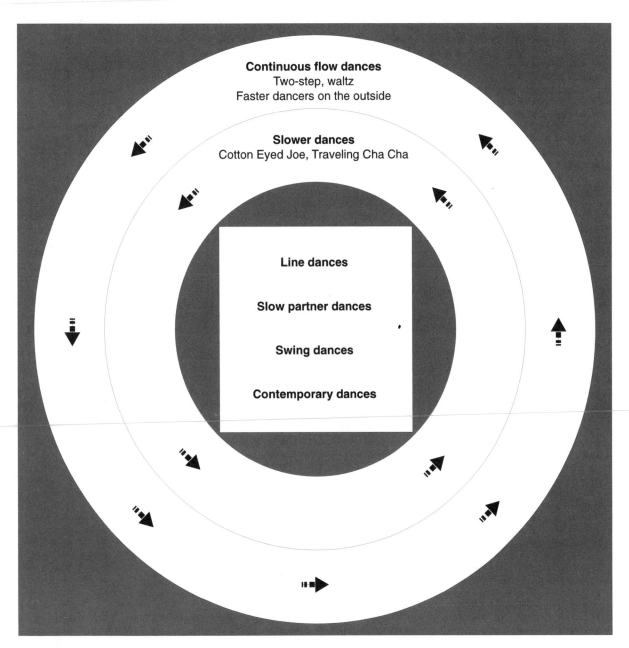

Figure 1.1 Dance floor etiquette.

Stop—close your eyes and feel this position. Practice this little exercise for good body awareness. Lift your chin so it is parallel to the floor. Are you biting your tongue? Wiggle your fingers so I know you are relaxed. Now, walk forward away from the wall and see if you can maintain your posture. Don't look down! Looking at your feet while dancing will only make you dizzy, and you will miss the wonderful scenery. Now practice walking backward, at your own pace. Try walking forward and back taking smaller steps, and keep your knees close together while moving.

Did you ever get in trouble when you were a kid for standing around and putting your hands in your pockets? Well, no more—this is your chance! The standard arm position for guys in line dancing is thumbs in the pockets or on the belt, and for the women it is a relaxed fist at waist or hip level. It is also acceptable to have relaxed arms by your sides. Even though these are the standard arm positions, it is becoming more popular to freestyle your arms to express your own personality. However, standard arm positions are good practice when you are first learning. Go ahead now and try walking with your arms in either one of the positions. You're on a roll!

Look Good

Lookin' good may give you that extra "boot" you need to make you feel better on the dance floor. The clothing style for line dancing depends on the area in which you live and on you. If your environment is country, the country-western dances are influenced by the cowboy boots and cowboy hats. Check the yellow pages for a local country-western store near you, and take the time to learn about the appropriate up-to-date styles. Also, you can visit the Internet for ideas on what to wear.

There is actually a right and a wrong way to buy a cowboy hat. Never buy one too small or tight. Buy it a little large so that it will fit even when your hair grows. To tighten the fit of a loose hat, unfold the inside band and insert some sticky foam tape. You can easily remove the tape later, if necessary.

Shoes are the most valuable "gear" for dancing. Just as you need good skis to ski, good shoes are definitely an asset with line dancing! Wear footwear that slides and swivels easily and doesn't stick to the floor. Suede and leather soles are usually the best. Avoid boots that have synthetic lining. Synthetic lining does not breathe or stretch as well as natural leather and tends to crack and tear over time. If you are in a health club or environment that requires an athletic shoe, you may want to purchase a cross-training aerobic shoe rather than a running shoe. Just remember to pick up your feet more as you dance so that you don't injure your knees by trying to turn with heavy rubber soles. And be careful on slippery floors.

Actually, since line dancing today is performed to so many styles of music, just about any clothing is suitable. (Now, don't take me too literally!) And, of course, good hygiene, confidence, and a smile do wonders!

Listen to the Music

So you say you don't have rhythm? Hogwash! Everyone has rhythm—some just listen to the music differently, that's all. So what is rhythm? Let's just say it is your subconscious coming out to play with your conscious for a while.

Here's an idea to help with your rhythm. Try counting the beats per minute to a song. What is the beat of the song? It is the beat you subconsciously tap your foot to when you listen to the music. Your subconscious hears it beautifully. All you need to do is to tell your conscious to listen to it.

If you were to count the taps of your foot for a full minute, you would end up with the beats per minute (BPM) of that song. Try clapping your hands to the beat of music in counts of eight. Then try walking a step to each beat. Slower songs are easier to dance to, and you will discover that they are about 90 to 110 BPM. Medium tempo songs are about 120 to 140 BPM, and advanced dances are 150 or more BPM.

Now try walking two steps to each beat. As you do this, concentrate on relaxing. Let your intuition take over—it understands the music. Next, try putting on a waltz, and clap and walk to a count of six beats instead of eight. Then forget about walking and just let your body move naturally—go with the flow. This exercise will prove to you that you do have and feel rhythm!

So what dances go with what songs? There is a suggested music list for each dance in this book for your enjoyment. However, keep in mind that you can dance any line dance to many songs. Some line dances were created just for a particular song, but soon you will get a feel for the style of the dance and which songs go best with it. There is no set rule as to which dance goes with which song. It is all a matter of personal preference. Usually at dance clubs, someone will start a line dance and others fall in and follow their new "leader." Yes, you may be a "leader" someday. So practice line dancing to various music—especially songs you really enjoy.

Have Fun

Line dancing is a great stress reducer! The benefits are enormous. First, you cannot possibly think of anything else when your mind is on memorizing steps. What a great way to take your mind off _____ (you fill in the blank). Line dancing can be an emotional release, especially when you let yourself go with the music. It is also good exercise, just like low-impact aerobics. Speaking of aerobics, many health clubs around the country today are teaching line dancing. Line dancing is a great way to blend exercise and recreation because you can raise your heart rate up to 60 to 70 percent of its maximum, which builds stamina safely. All you have to do to achieve an aerobic benefit is to gradually increase the amount of time that you dance continuously. Start with one song and gradually add others until you are dancing 15 to 60 minutes nonstop three times per week. The best part about line dancing is that it is a super way to meet new people and experience great personal satisfaction from your accomplishments.

Okay, so do we have our mental act together? Are you standing tall? Are you breathing? Are you thinking positively? Well then, let's do it!

Know
Your Lingo

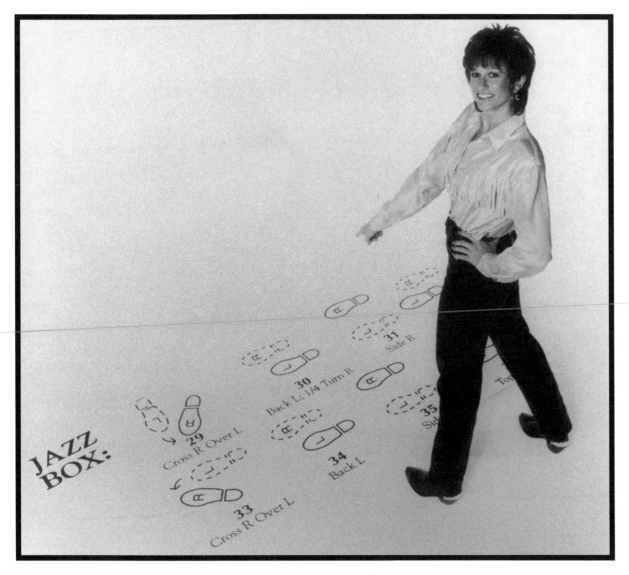

Before you hit the dance floor to practice the steps you'll find in the following chapters, there are a few things you should know—most importantly, how to read the foot maps and understand the lingo in which they are written. This chapter will help you out in these all-important areas.

How to Read a Foot Map

Reading a foot map is very similar to reading a road map, so long as you know what direction you are going and what all those little symbols mean. When you see an arrow, follow the direction it is pointing. It's that easy. The following key defines all the symbols on the foot maps. For example, the foot pictured with a solid line is just like the solid line on a freeway map. It's the best way to go, so put your weight on it. And the rest stops are even illustrated for you. Of course, the rest stops in this book are slightly different from the ones on a road map. They are easily marked by the word "hold," and that's exactly what you do—nothing. (These rests are great opportunities to "get your head together" for the next step.)

Have a look here at an example of your dancing road map and the key to symbols.

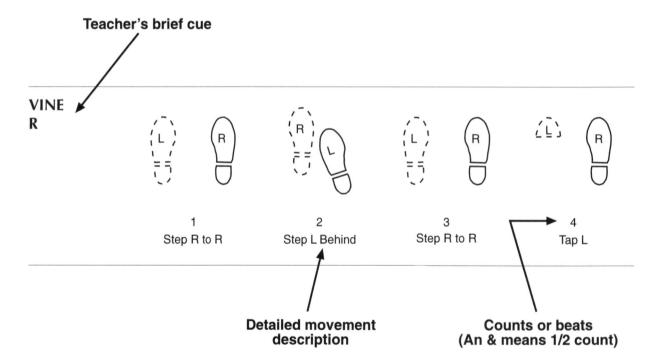

Key to Symbols

Symbol	Meaning	Symbol	Meaning
	One-quarter turn		Scuff
	One-half turn		Tap toe twice
&	Half count		Jump
R	Right		
L	Left		
	Weight on foot		Hop
	No weight on foot		Stomp, changing weight to foot
	Weight on ball of foot		Stomp, rebounding foot off floor
	No weight on ball of the foot (tap or touch)		
	Weight on heel of foot		Scoot or chug
	No weight on heel of foot (tap or touch)		
	Clap hands		Hitch or hook
	Kick (or brush) foot forward		
	Tap heel twice		Lift knee

Line Dancing Terminology

Want to make an impression the next time you go dancing? Try using lingo such as "grapevines," "scoots," "swivels," and "hooks," then suggest how well everyone does the "hitch kick" and see what happens. The lingo to assist you in learning your dances is listed below. Maybe you can write a few terms on the palm of your hand in case you need a quick reference next time you are out on the town! Good luck!

accent—Special emphasis to a movement or a heavy beat in music.

and—Half of a count or a quick count. For example, "one and two" or "and one two." Noted in foot maps with an ampersand (&).

ball change—A change of weight from the ball of one foot to the ball of the other foot (see photos on page 109).

begin—The start of the dance.

BPM—Beats per minute. The number of beats of music in one minute.

brush—A brushing or sweeping movement of the ball of the foot against the floor (see photo on page 165).

ccw—When used in step directions, it refers to counterclockwise.

center—The dancer's balancing point in proper alignment, usually meaning the weight is on both feet together with the toes pointing forward. Also known as *starting point*.

cha-cha—Five steps to four beats of music beginning with either the left or right foot. This step can move forward, backward, or from side to side in either direction. The rhythm is slow, slow, quick, quick, slow. Usually performed with hip action. For example:

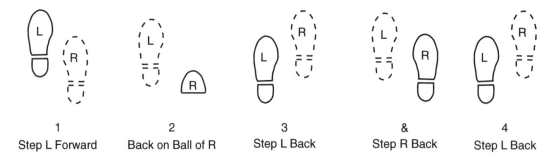

1	2	3	&	4
Step L Forward	Back on Ball of R	Step L Back	Step R Back	Step L Back

chaîné turn—See *three-step turn*. Can be performed in multiples.

charleston—A four-step pattern with four beats. For example:

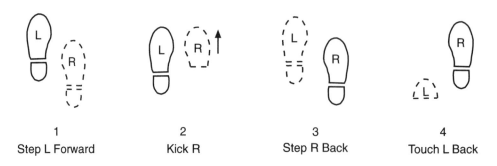

1	2	3	4
Step L Forward	Kick R	Step R Back	Touch L Back

chassé—A three-step pattern performed to two beats of music. Similar to a triple-step, only it can move forward, backward, or from side to side in either direction. The free foot never passes the supporting foot.

choreography—The arranging or planning of dance movements into routines.

chug—Traveling in the air while hopping on the supporting leg forward, backward, or sideways with the other leg in a hitch position. Also known as a *scoot*. (See photo on page 97.)

clockwise—See *reverse line of dance (RLOD)*.

close—To bring feet together without a change of weight.

cross—Crossing anything in front or behind of the other.

CW—An abbreviation for country-western.

cw—When used in step directions, it refers to clockwise.

diagonal—A movement left or right at 45 degrees from center, facing one wall.

dig—Touching the ball or heel of the nonsupporting foot with a strong emphasis.

dip—A slight bend of the supporting knee, keeping the other knee straight.

drag—To bring the nonsupporting free foot slowly together to the supporting foot in a sliding or dragging movement. Also known as a *slide* or *draw*.

draw—See *drag*.

fan—A circular motion of the free foot close to the ground.

fan kick—A circular motion of the free foot in the air.

follow-through—The nonsupporting foot passes by the weighted foot before changing directions.

grapevine—A three-count traveling move performed side to side and often finished with a fourth count that is a touch, brush, kick, or similar step. Also referred to as a *vine*. The second step crosses in back. (See photos on page 57.) Turning instead of stepping is called a *three-step turn* or *rolling grapevine*. For example:

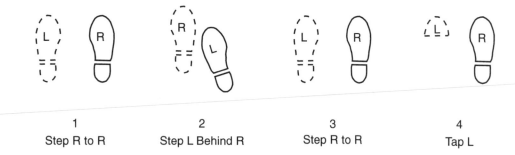

1	2	3	4
Step R to R	Step L Behind R	Step R to R	Tap L

half-turn—See *pivot turn*.

heel—Tap the floor with the heel of the foot (see photo on page 152).

heel fan—With feet together, rotate one heel out and return to center, keeping toes together. For example:

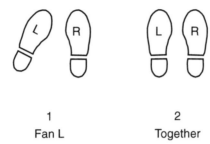

1	2
Fan L	Together

heel pivot—A turn on the heel of one foot with no weight change.

heel splits—With feet together and weight on the balls of both feet, push both heels apart on count 1 and bring heels together on count 2 (see photos on page 83). Usually performed in two counts. However, in some very fast dances, it can be performed in one count. Also known as *pigeon toe*.

heel stomps—Stomp the heels to the floor with a rapid motion.

hip bump—An emphasized hip movement in any given direction. (See photos on page 168.)

hip roll—Bend the knees slightly and make a circle with the hips.

hitch—Lift foot off the ground, bending slightly at the knee. The height of the knee is determined by personal preference. (See photo on page 24.)

hitch kick—See *kick ball change*.

hitch turn—Hitch and turn together using hitch momentum to carry through turn.

hold—Counting off a designated time or number of beats before taking another step.

hook—The action of lifting the foot off the ground with the knee bent and crossing in front and below the knee of the supporting leg. (See photo on page 118.)

hook turn—A 360-degree turn performed on the ball of one foot. Also known as a *pirouette* or *spin*.

hop—Start with weight on supporting foot, spring into the air, and land on same foot.

jazz box—This is a four-count move with four weight changes and can be performed to the left or right. Step in each corner of an imaginary box on the floor. Some dances start with step 2 and end with step 1. (See photos on page 91.) Also known as a *jazz square*. For example:

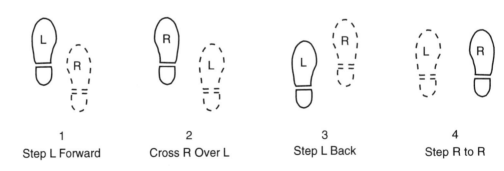

1	2	3	4
Step L Forward	Cross R Over L	Step L Back	Step R to R

jazz square—See *jazz box.*

jump—With the weight on both feet, spring into the air and land on both feet.

kick—Lift the nonsupporting leg from the knee and straighten the knee; usually performed with a flexed foot.

kick ball change—Kick forward with one leg, then place weight on the ball of the foot of that same leg and change weight immediately to the other foot. It takes two counts of music for the three steps; usually performed to "1 & 2." (See photos on page 128.)

knee dip—Bend and straighten both knees.

leap—With the weight on one foot, jump into the air and land on the other foot.

line of dance (LOD)—The counterclockwise circular movement of dancers around the dance floor. Dancing in a clockwise direction is called *reverse line of dance (RLOD).*

lindy—A combination of steps traveling either right or left consisting of a triple step and ball change. For example, a right lindy is: step R to R, step L together, step R to R, step on the ball of the L foot behind the R, step R in place.

lock—A tight cross of the feet.

military half-turn—See *pivot turn.*

military turn—A four-count turn consisting of two pivot turns performed together in the same direction. For example, a right military turn consists of stepping forward on R and turning 180 degrees L and stepping onto L. Then step forward on R again, and turn 180 degrees L and step onto L. One military turn equals two pivot turns combined.

over—To step across in front of the weighted foot.

paddle turn—A turn either left or right using a series of ball changes with three-quarters of the weight staying on the turning foot. The other foot executes a pushing movement to make the quarter-, half-, three-quarter or full turn.

pas de bourrée—See *sailor steps.*

pigeon toe—See *heel splits.*

pirouette—See *spin.*

pivot turn— A two-count turn also known as a *military half-turn.* For example, a pivot turn left consists of stepping forward on R and turning 180 degrees to L and stepping onto L foot. (See photos on page 115.)

plié—A bend of the knees.

point—Stretching the toes of the free foot so the foot "points" forward, backward, sideways, or crosswise. Usually ends in a tap or touch.

polka step—Similar to a *triple-step* or *shuffle*, but done in a more bouncy and lively style with the feet farther off the floor.

quarter-turn—A 90-degree turn to the left or right.

reverse line of dance (RLOD)—The clockwise circular movement of dancers around the dance floor.

rock—Shifting the weight from foot to foot. Sometimes referred to as *sway.*

rolling grapevine—See *three-step turn.*

sailor steps—Also known as a *pas de bourrée*. This is a three-step shuffle pattern to two beats of music, consisting of crossing one foot behind the other, stepping to one side, then stepping to the other side. The body leans slightly side to side in opposition of the weighted foot. For example:

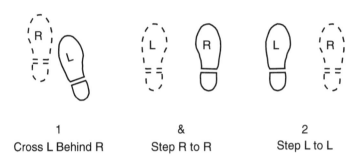

1	&	2
Cross L Behind R	Step R to R	Step L to L

scoot—Hop on the same foot while traveling forward, backward, or sideways with the nonsupporting leg in a hook position. Also known as a *chug*.

scuff—A sweeping movement of the heel of the foot against the floor. (See photo on page 24.)

shimmy—Moving the shoulders alternately forward and back.

shuffle—Three steps performed forward or backward to two beats of music, usually counted "1 & 2." The second step can either place the free foot beside the supporting foot (sometimes described by teachers as step-together-step) or the ball of the free foot next to the arch of the supporting foot. Also known as a *triple-step*.

slide—Step on one foot and draw the nonsupporting foot up to the supporting foot in a dragging movement. (See photos on page 55.)

spin—A 360-degree turn on one foot. Also known as *pirouette*.

spiral turn—Cross one foot behind the other. Keeping feet in place, rotate body 180 degrees for a half spiral turn or 360 degrees for a full spiral turn.

spotting—A technique used to avoid dizziness resulting from a series of fast turns. Focus your eyes on a spot for as long as possible when turning. Rotate your head after your body begins turning, completing the head rotation before your body finishes the turn.

step—Transfer weight from one foot to the other.

stomp—Hit the floor with the whole foot or heel. Either change weight onto that foot or rebound the foot without changing weight and use the same foot for the next movement. (See photos on page 160.)

strut—A two-count walk performed by stepping on the heel, then the entire foot of the same leg.

swing—Raise the free foot and move it forward, backward, to the side, or crosswise.

switch—A quick shift of weight from one foot to the other. For example, put one heel forward and in one beat perform a small hop and switch to the other heel forward. (See photos on page 88.)

swivel—With feet together, turn on the balls of the foot right or left and rotate hips side to side (see photos on page 35). The upper body is stationary while hips and heels rotate. For example:

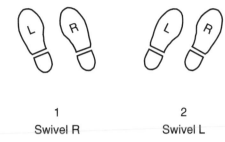

1
Swivel R

2
Swivel L

tap or touch—The toe of the free foot taps or touches the floor without a weight change (see photo on page 48). For example:

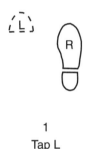

1
Tap L

tempo—Speed of the beat of music.

three-step turn—A traveling 360-degree turn on the balls of the feet. Take three steps to complete the turn and end with a tap, step, point, scuff, or kick. When starting on the right foot, turn to the right. Can be done in multiples. Also known as a *rolling grapevine* or a *chaîné turn.*

toe fan—With feet together, rotate one toe out and return to center, keeping heels together. (See photos on page 157.) For example:

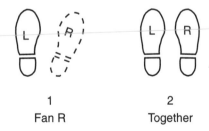

1
Fan R

2
Together

toe splits—With feet together and weight on heels of both feet, push toes apart on count 1. Bring toes together on count 2. (See photos on page 136.) Also known as *scissor splits.*

toe strut—Same as a *strut,* only step with toe and then heel.

together—Bring feet together sometimes with the weight evenly distributed on both feet, and sometimes with the weight only on one foot.

triple-step—See *shuffle.*

turn—A rotation of the body, taking one or more steps to complete.

variations—Movements of footwork that vary from the indicated dance patterns while maintaining the same count.

vine—See *grapevine.*

walk—Two or more steps forward, backward, or to the side.

weave—A continuous grapevine of six or more counts, sometimes referred to as a *traveling grapevine.*

Heel, Toe, Heel, Toe— Here We Go!

Beginning Line Dances

Okay, here we go. Let's start with some beginning line dances. What makes a line dance suitable for beginners? The first consideration is the length of the dance (the total number of steps). The dances in this chapter are 16 to 42 counts, and most finish in multiples of 8 counts. It is easy to repeat the sequence at the end of an 8 count (or phrase) because we naturally count beats of music in eights. Another reason these dances are considered easier is because they are usually performed to slower-tempo songs. Also, most of the steps are performed in one beat of music as opposed to more intricate steps in the intermediate and advanced dances, which sometimes have two steps to one beat of music. You will also notice that beginning dances have limited changes of direction during the basic movement pattern.

Learn one dance at a time; go at your own pace; and practice, practice, practice. Remember that a few steps performed well are better than several steps performed sloppily. And a pointer about music: be sure to select a slow pace when you are first learning a dance. Then change to a faster pace once you have mastered it. Your homework for this week is practical application. So go out and try the dances!

Bus Stop	29	Electric Slide II	54
Chattahoochee	38	Flying Eight	56
Cowboy Boogie	25	Freeze	23
Cowboy Hustle	40	Hitchhiker	62
Cowboy Macarena	62	Louie	46
Cowboy Motion	21	One Step Forward, Two Steps Back	52
Cowgirl's Twist	31	Reggae Cowboy	58
Coyote	42	Slappin' Leather	49
Double Dutch Bus	34	Smooth	36
Down and Dirty	44	Tennessee Twister	60
Electric Slide I	27		

Cowboy Motion

This dance appeared on our national survey in almost every state when it was first released. One of the easiest dances, Cowboy Motion is most fun when performed to fast music.

Music Suggestions

"Have Mercy" by The Judds

"I Feel Lucky" by Mary Chapin Carpenter

"Whatcha Gonna Do With a Cowboy" by Chris LeDoux

Step Descriptions

1-4	Grapevine R (step R to R, cross L behind R, step R to R), tap L
5-8	Grapevine L (step L to L, cross L behind R, step L to L), tap R
9-12	Walk back R, L, R, stomp L
13-16	Tap L toe to L side twice, tap L heel forward twice
17-20	Tap L toe to L, tap L heel forward, switch feet ending with R heel forward, clap hands
21-24	Rock weight forward over R, rock back, rock forward, rock back and one-quarter turn L

Variations

1. On counts 4 and 8, replace the tap with a scuff.

2. On counts 21 to 24, bump hips twice forward and twice backward instead of rocking.

Foot Map

VINE R

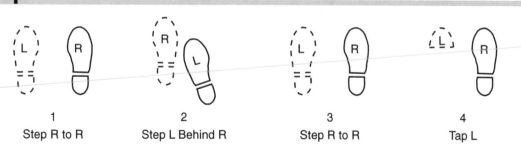

1	2	3	4
Step R to R	Step L Behind R	Step R to R	Tap L

(continued)

Cowboy Motion *(continued)*

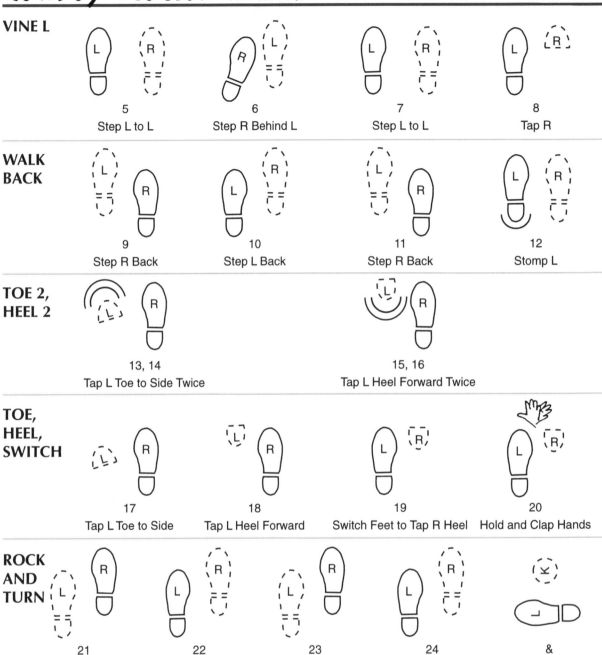

VINE L

5	6	7	8
Step L to L	Step R Behind L	Step L to L	Tap R

WALK BACK

9	10	11	12
Step R Back	Step L Back	Step R Back	Stomp L

TOE 2, HEEL 2

13, 14	15, 16
Tap L Toe to Side Twice	Tap L Heel Forward Twice

TOE, HEEL, SWITCH

17	18	19	20
Tap L Toe to Side	Tap L Heel Forward	Switch Feet to Tap R Heel	Hold and Clap Hands

ROCK AND TURN

21	22	23	24	&
Step R Forward and Rock R	Rock Back Onto L	Rock Forward Onto R	Rock Back Onto L	Lift R Knee and 1/4 Turn L

Freeze

The Freeze is similar to the Electric Slide. One source says its name came from one part of the earlier version of the Freeze where someone would shout "freeze 2, 3, 4" on counts 13, 14, 15, and 16. All of the dancers would stop during those counts and thus figuratively "freeze!"

Music Suggestions

"Elvira" by the Oak Ridge Boys

"I Feel Lucky" by Mary Chapin Carpenter

"Third Rock From the Sun" by Joe Diffie

Step Descriptions

1-4   Grapevine R (step R to R, cross L behind R, step R to R), tap L

5-8   Grapevine L (step L to L, cross R behind L, step L to L), tap R

9-12   Walk back R, L, R, hitch L

13-16   Step L forward (slight lean forward), rock back onto R, rock forward onto L, scuff R and one-quarter turn L

Variations

1. Replace counts 1 to 3 with a three-step turn to the R and counts 5 to 7 with a three-step turn to the L.

2. Substitute the foot movement in counts 4, 8, and 12 with a kick, brush, hop, or scoot.

3. Replace the walk back in counts 9 to 11 with a three-step turn to the back.

4. Hitch instead of scuff on count 16.

Foot Map

VINE R

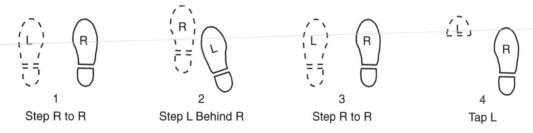

1	2	3	4
Step R to R	Step L Behind R	Step R to R	Tap L

(continued)

Freeze (continued)

VINE L

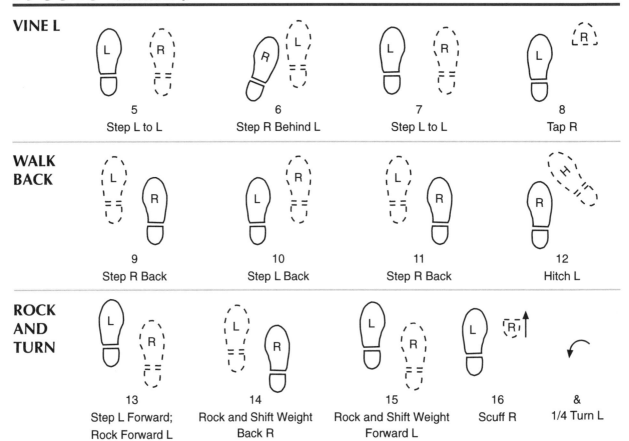

5	6	7	8
Step L to L	Step R Behind L	Step L to L	Tap R

WALK BACK

9	10	11	12
Step R Back	Step L Back	Step R Back	Hitch L

ROCK AND TURN

13	14	15	16	&
Step L Forward; Rock Forward L	Rock and Shift Weight Back R	Rock and Shift Weight Forward L	Scuff R	1/4 Turn L

Hitch

Lift foot, bend knee.

Scuff

Sweep heel against floor.

Cowboy Boogie

You should learn this dance after the Freeze but before the Electric Slide since the steps are so similar.

Music Suggestions

"Elvira" by the Oak Ridge Boys

"Dumas Walker" by the Kentucky Headhunters

"Cowboy Boogie" by Randy Travis

Step Descriptions

1-4   Grapevine R (step R to R, cross L behind R, step R to R), kick L

5-8   Grapevine L (step L to L, cross R behind L, step L to L), kick R

9-12   Step R forward, scuff L, step L forward, scuff R

13-16   Walk back R, L, R, hitch L

17-20   Step L forward, tap R next to L, step R back, tap L next to R

21-24   Step L forward, shift weight to R, shift weight to L, scuff R foot and one-quarter turn L

Variations

1. On counts 9 to 12, substitute the scuffs with holds, hops, or hip bumps.

2. On counts 17 to 20, add hip bumps while stepping and tapping.

Foot Map

VINE R

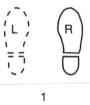 

1	2	3	4
Step R to R	Step L Behind R	Step R to R	Kick L

(continued)

Cowboy Boogie (continued)

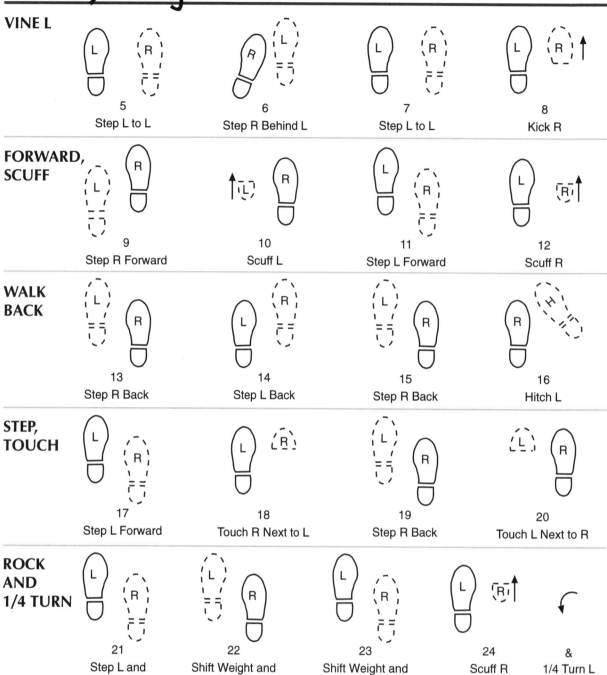

VINE L

5	6	7	8
Step L to L	Step R Behind L	Step L to L	Kick R

FORWARD, SCUFF

9	10	11	12
Step R Forward	Scuff L	Step L Forward	Scuff R

WALK BACK

13	14	15	16
Step R Back	Step L Back	Step R Back	Hitch L

STEP, TOUCH

17	18	19	20
Step L Forward	Touch R Next to L	Step R Back	Touch L Next to R

ROCK AND 1/4 TURN

21	22	23	24	&
Step L and Rock Forward	Shift Weight and Rock Back to R	Shift Weight and Rock Forward to L	Scuff R	1/4 Turn L

Electric Slide I

This dance was originally choreographed beginning with a slide to the right and then the left. However, during the years, the slide movement has been modified to a grapevine right and then left. Either way is right! Try the Electric Slide I and II (see page 54) to different types of music. Probably the most popular line dance today, both young and old enjoy doing it at parties, weddings, and social events because it can be done to many other types of music besides country.

Music Suggestions

"Electric Slide" on *Christy Lane's Guide to Party Dances*

"Electric Boogie" by Marcia Griffiths

"Funky Cowboy" by Ronnie McDowell

Step Descriptions

1-4   Step R to R, slide L to R, step R to R, slide L to R, step R to R, stomp L

5-8   Step L to L, slide R to L, step L to L, slide R to L, step L to L, stomp R

9-12   Walk back R, L, R, tap L next to R and clap hands

13-16 Step L forward, touch R next to L, step R back, touch L next to R

17-18 Step L forward, brush R as pivot one-quarter turn to L

Variations

1. Replace counts 1 to 4 and 5 to 8 with either a grapevine or a three-step turn and stomp.

2. On counts 9 to 12, replace walks with a three-step turn rotating R and traveling back.

3. On count 12, replace tap L with jump feet together and out.

4. On counts 13 to 16, step L forward into a lunge and slap ground, step R back and high-kick L.

5. On counts 17 to 18, replace one-quarter turn with full turn L.

6. You can modify this dance so that it ends in 16 counts by eliminating one of the slides (counts 1 and 2) after performing the entire dance once through.

Electric Slide I *(continued)*

Foot Map

SLIDE R

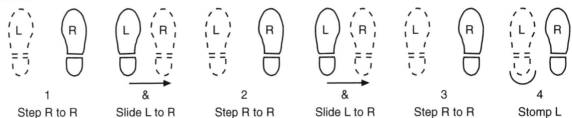

1	&	2	&	3	4
Step R to R	Slide L to R	Step R to R	Slide L to R	Step R to R	Stomp L

SLIDE L

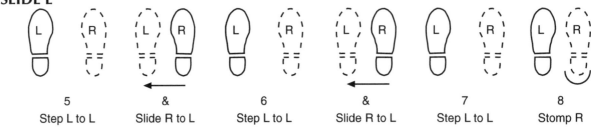

5	&	6	&	7	8
Step L to L	Slide R to L	Step L to L	Slide R to L	Step L to L	Stomp R

WALK BACK

9	10	11	12
Step R Back	Step L Back	Step R Back	Tap L; Clap Hands

STEP TOUCH

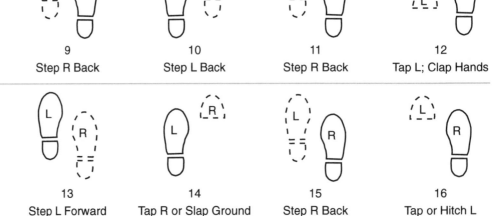

13	14	15	16
Step L Forward	Tap R or Slap Ground	Step R Back	Tap or Hitch L

FORWARD, BRUSH, AND TURN

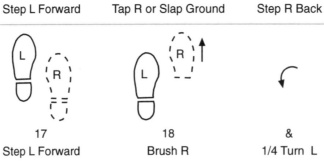

17	18	&
Step L Forward	Brush R	1/4 Turn L

Bus Stop

This line dance grew in popularity in the '70s during the disco craze. Try this dance to different styles of music, such as country, funk, disco, techno, and even Big Band!

Music Suggestions

"Get Up, Get Down, Get Funky, Get Loose" by Teddy Pendergrass

"Some Kind of Trouble" by Tanya Tucker

"Stayin' Alive" by the Bee Gees

Step Descriptions

1-4	Walk back R, L, R, tap L
5-8	Walk forward L, R, L, tap R
9-12	Grapevine R (step R to R, cross L behind R, step R to R), tap L
13-16	Grapevine L (step L to L, cross R behind L, step L to L), tap R
17-20	Step R to R, tap L next to R, step L to L, tap R next to L
21-24	Step R to R, slide L together, heel splits out, heels together
25-28	Tap R forward twice, tap R backward twice
29-32	Tap R forward, tap R back, tap R side, one-quarter turn L, stomp R

Variations

1. On counts 17 to 20, jump forward and shake hips for two counts, jump back and shake hips for two counts. On counts 21 to 24, jump forward one count, jump back one count, click heels twice.

2. Start the dance on count 9 instead of count 1 and continue all the way through for the entire 32 counts.

Foot Map

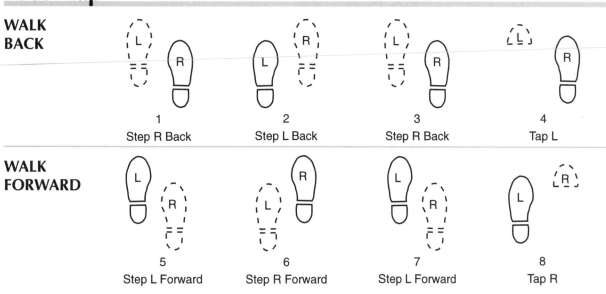

WALK BACK

1	2	3	4
Step R Back	Step L Back	Step R Back	Tap L

WALK FORWARD

5	6	7	8
Step L Forward	Step R Forward	Step L Forward	Tap R

(continued)

Bus Stop (continued)

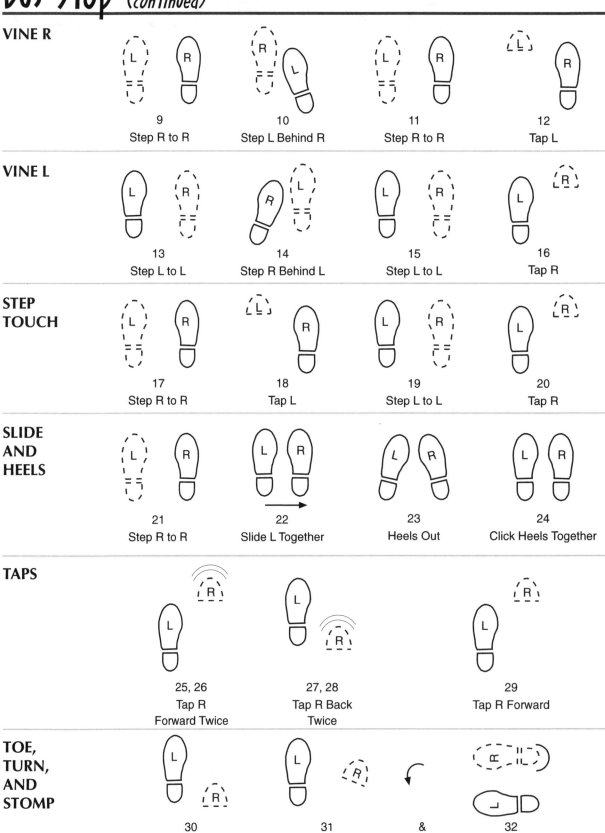

VINE R

9	10	11	12
Step R to R	Step L Behind R	Step R to R	Tap L

VINE L

13	14	15	16
Step L to L	Step R Behind L	Step L to L	Tap R

STEP TOUCH

17	18	19	20
Step R to R	Tap L	Step L to L	Tap R

SLIDE AND HEELS

21	22	23	24
Step R to R	Slide L Together	Heels Out	Click Heels Together

TAPS

25, 26	27, 28	29
Tap R Forward Twice	Tap R Back Twice	Tap R Forward

TOE, TURN, AND STOMP

30	31	&	32
Tap R Back	Tap R to Side	1/4 Turn L	Stomp R

Cowgirl's Twist

Try dancing this line dance to any "twist" music from Chubby Checker to Ronnie McDowell.

Music Suggestions

"Rockin' With the Rhythm of the Rain" by The Judds

"What the Cowgirls Do" by Vince Gill

"Any Man of Mine" by Shania Twain

Step Descriptions

1-4	Strut forward R, L (touch R heel forward, snap down R toe, touch L heel forward, snap down L toe)
5-8	Repeat counts 1-4
9-12	Walk back R, L, R, step L next to R
13-16	Swivel both heels L, swivel both toes L, swivel both heels L, hold (the swivels travel to the L)
17-20	Swivel both heels R, swivel both toes R, swivel both heels R, hold (the swivels travel to the R)

21-24	Swivel both heels L, hold, swivel both heels R, hold
25-28	Swivel both heels L, swivel both heels R, bring heels to center, hold
29-32	Step R forward and lean R shoulder forward, hold, one-quarter turn L and step L, as lean L shoulder forward, hold

Variation

Clap hands on all the "holds."

Foot Map

STRUT

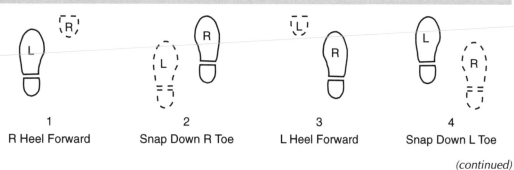

1	2	3	4
R Heel Forward	Snap Down R Toe	L Heel Forward	Snap Down L Toe

(continued)

Cowgirl's Twist (continued)

STRUT

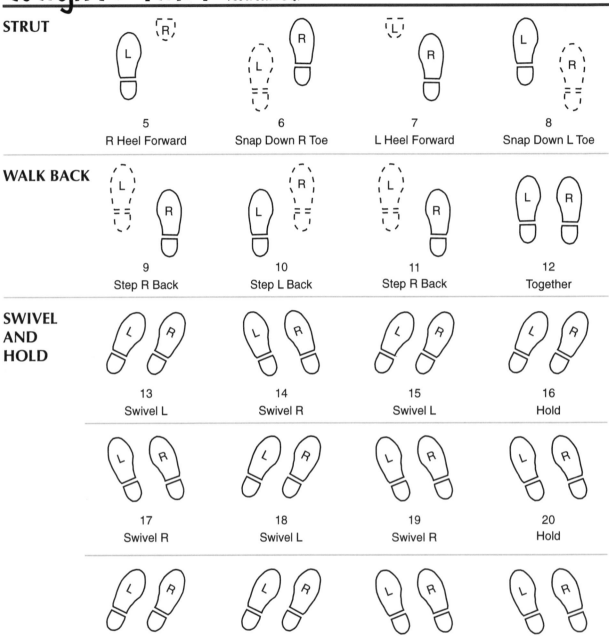

5	6	7	8
R Heel Forward	Snap Down R Toe	L Heel Forward	Snap Down L Toe

WALK BACK

9	10	11	12
Step R Back	Step L Back	Step R Back	Together

SWIVEL AND HOLD

13	14	15	16
Swivel L	Swivel R	Swivel L	Hold

17	18	19	20
Swivel R	Swivel L	Swivel R	Hold

21	22	23	24
Swivel L	Hold	Swivel R	Hold

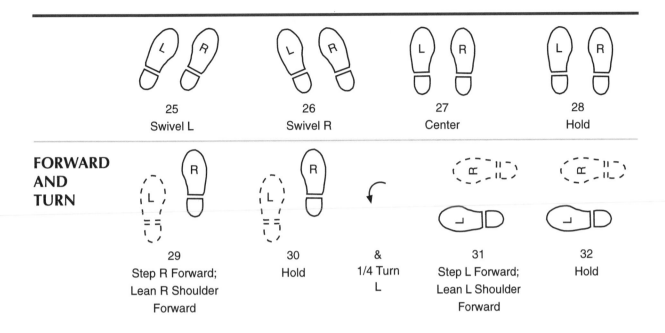

25 Swivel L	26 Swivel R	27 Center	28 Hold

FORWARD AND TURN

29 Step R Forward; Lean R Shoulder Forward	30 Hold	& 1/4 Turn L	31 Step L Forward; Lean L Shoulder Forward	32 Hold

Strut

R heel forward.

Snap down R toe.

Double Dutch Bus

This dance was originally choreographed to the song "Double Dutch Bus" by Frankie Smith. You will need to start on the "&" count.

Music Suggestions

"Double Dutch Bus" by Frankie Smith

"Call of the Wild" by Aaron Tippin

"Drive South" by Suzy Bogguss

Step Descriptions

&1-2   Step R forward, step L next to R, hold

&3-4   Step R back, step L next to R, hold

5-8   Roll (circle) R knee to R twice, roll (circle) L knee to L twice

9-12   Tap R to R, feet together, tap L to L, feet together

13-14   Swivel L, return to center

15-18   R heel forward twice, tap R toe back twice

19-22   R heel forward with weight on R heel, one-quarter turn L and step L forward, R heel forward, R toe back

23-26   Step R forward, hold, drag L to R, feet together

Variation

For counts 1 to 4, substitute a hop on the R forward and hold, and hop on the R backward and hold.

Foot Map

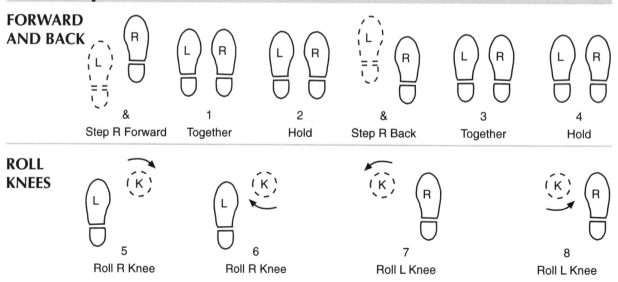

34

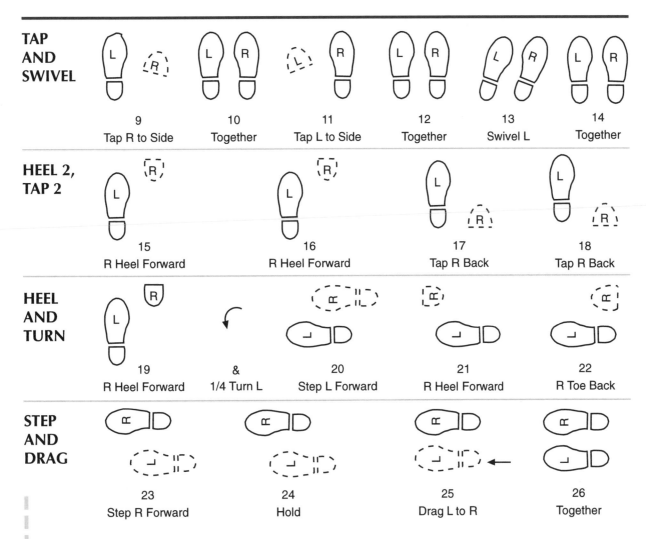

TAP AND SWIVEL	9 Tap R to Side	10 Together	11 Tap L to Side	12 Together	13 Swivel L	14 Together

HEEL 2, TAP 2	15 R Heel Forward	16 R Heel Forward	17 Tap R Back	18 Tap R Back

HEEL AND TURN	19 R Heel Forward	& 1/4 Turn L	20 Step L Forward	21 R Heel Forward	22 R Toe Back

STEP AND DRAG	23 Step R Forward	24 Hold	25 Drag L to R	26 Together

Turn on balls of feet; heels move L or R.

 **Smooth**

Interestingly, some dancers stop this dance at 28 counts and then repeat it from the top. It is much easier to count in eights, so that is probably why there is another version. Learn the entire dance; you can always cut it off at 28 counts if you wish.

Music Suggestions

"Smooth" by the Kentucky Headhunters

"Outbound Plane" by Suzy Bogguss

"Super Love" by Exile

Step Descriptions

1-4   Touch R toe forward, touch R toe next to L, touch R toe to R, step R next to L

5-8   Touch L toe forward, touch L toe next to R, touch L toe to L, touch L toe next to R

9-12   Grapevine L (step L to L, cross R behind L, step L to L), scuff R

13-16   Grapevine R (step R to R, cross L behind R, step R to R), scuff L

17-20   Step L forward, drag R foot behind L and step R, step L forward, scuff R

21-24   Step R forward, drag L foot behind R and step L, step R forward, scuff L

25-28   Step L forward, drag R foot behind L and step R, one-quarter turn L and step L, stomp R next to L, end with weight on both feet

29-32   Swivel heels to R, center, swivel heels to L, center

Variations

1.   On counts 1 and 5, touch the heel forward instead of the toe.

2.   On counts 29 to 32, replace swivel heels with heel splits.

Foot Map

TOUCH R

1	2	3	4
Touch R Forward	Touch R Next to L	Touch R to R	Step R Together

TOUCH L

5	6	7	8
Touch L Forward	Touch L Next to R	Touch L to L	Touch L Next to R

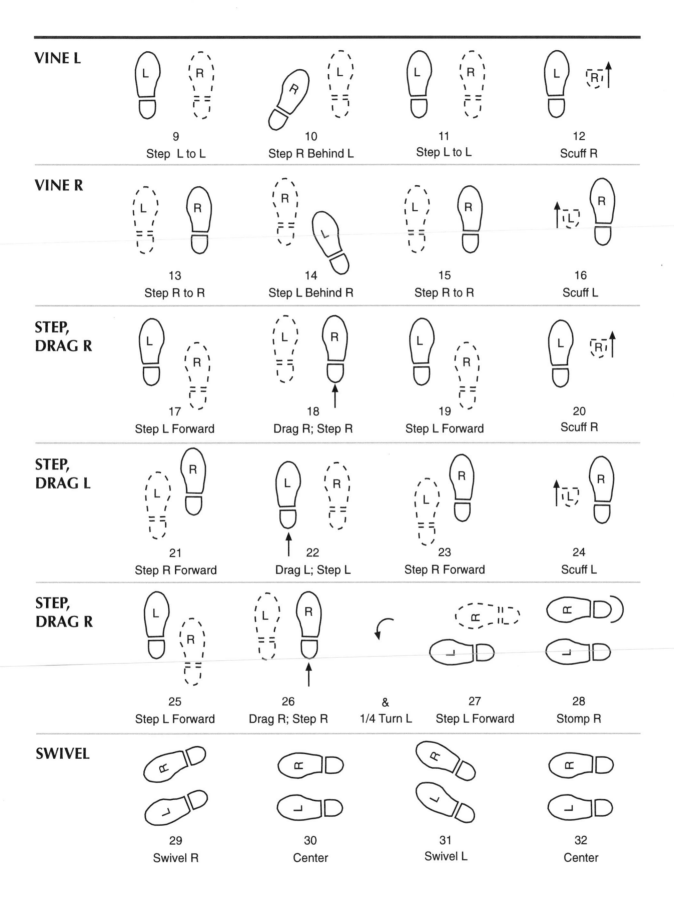

VINE L

9	10	11	12
Step L to L	Step R Behind L	Step L to L	Scuff R

VINE R

13	14	15	16
Step R to R	Step L Behind R	Step R to R	Scuff L

STEP, DRAG R

17	18	19	20
Step L Forward	Drag R; Step R	Step L Forward	Scuff R

STEP, DRAG L

21	22	23	24
Step R Forward	Drag L; Step L	Step R Forward	Scuff L

STEP, DRAG R

25	26	&	27	28
Step L Forward	Drag R; Step R	1/4 Turn L	Step L Forward	Stomp R

SWIVEL

29	30	31	32
Swivel R	Center	Swivel L	Center

Chattahoochee

These days it is common for a new dance to be choreographed to accompany a popular song. The Chattahoochee is one of these dances. Enjoy dancing it to Alan Jackson's "Chattahoochee" or other songs with a similar tempo, rhythm, and style.

Music Suggestions

"Chattahoochee" by Alan Jackson

"Sure Is Monday" by Mark Chesnutt

"Redneck Girl" by the Bellamy Brothers

Step Descriptions

1-4	Touch L heel forward, hook L leg in front of R, touch L heel forward, step L in place
5-8	Swivel heels L, center, L, center
9-12	Touch R heel forward, hook R leg in front of L, touch R heel forward, step R in place
13-16	Swivel heels R, center, R, center

17-20	Step R to R, lift L leg behind R and slap with R hand, step L to L, lift R leg behind L and slap with L hand
21-24	Grapevine R (step R to R, cross L behind R, step R to R), hitch L and one-quarter turn R
25-28	Walk back L, R, L, stomp R next to L, keeping weight on R

Variation

Replace counts 5 to 8 with a step R forward, pivot R, step R forward, pivot R.

Foot Map

HEEL, HOOK

1	2	3	4
L Heel Forward	Hitch L Over R	L Heel Forward	Step L Together

SWIVEL

5	6	7	8
Swivel L	Center	Swivel L	Center

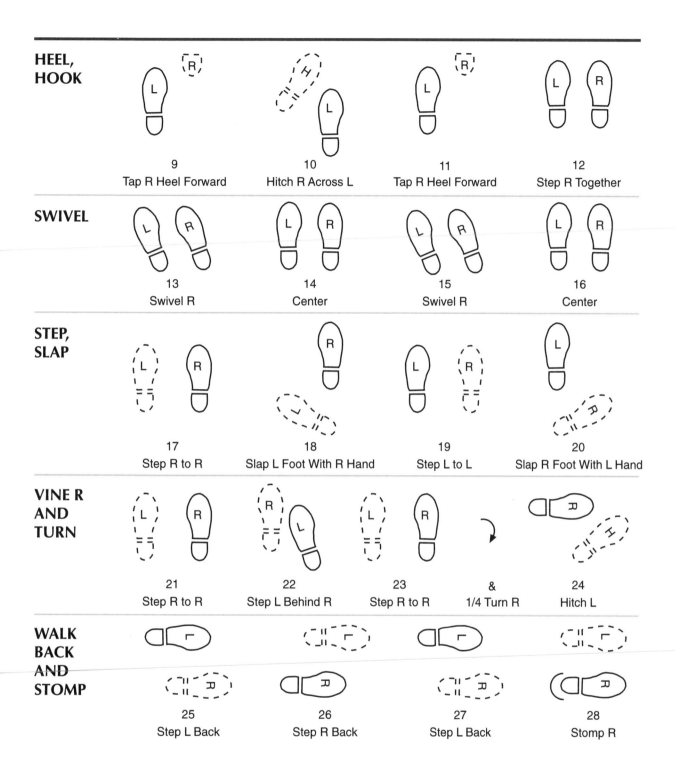

HEEL, HOOK

9	10	11	12
Tap R Heel Forward	Hitch R Across L	Tap R Heel Forward	Step R Together

SWIVEL

13	14	15	16
Swivel R	Center	Swivel R	Center

STEP, SLAP

17	18	19	20
Step R to R	Slap L Foot With R Hand	Step L to L	Slap R Foot With L Hand

VINE R AND TURN

21	22	23	&	24
Step R to R	Step L Behind R	Step R to R	1/4 Turn R	Hitch L

WALK BACK AND STOMP

25	26	27	28
Step L Back	Step R Back	Step L Back	Stomp R

Cowboy Hustle

This dance contains toe fans, taps, grapevines, and charleston kicks and is usually performed to medium-fast or fast music.

Music Suggestions

"Girls' Night Out" by The Judds

"Wrong Side of Memphis" by Trisha Yearwood

"Old Enough to Know Better" by Wade Hayes

Step Descriptions

1-4	Toe fan R, return toe center, toe fan R, return toe center
5-8	Tap R heel forward twice, tap R toe back twice
9-12	Tap R heel forward, tap R toe back, tap R heel forward, tap R toe back
13-16	Charleston (step R forward, kick L forward, step L back, tap R back)
17-20	Charleston (step R forward, kick L forward, step L back, touch R)
21-24	Grapevine R (step R to R, cross L behind R, step R to R), brush L
25-28	Step L to L, step R behind L, one-quarter turn L and step L, brush R
29-32	Step R forward, brush L, step L forward, stomp R next to L

Variation

On counts 21 to 24, replace with a rolling grapevine to the right.

Foot Map

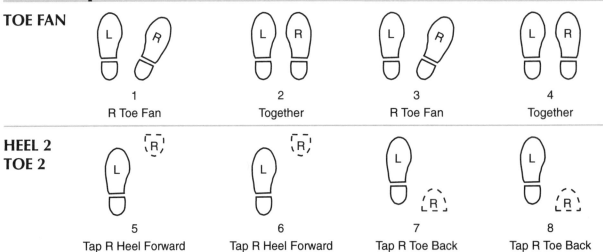

TOE FAN

1	2	3	4
R Toe Fan	Together	R Toe Fan	Together

HEEL 2 TOE 2

5	6	7	8
Tap R Heel Forward	Tap R Heel Forward	Tap R Toe Back	Tap R Toe Back

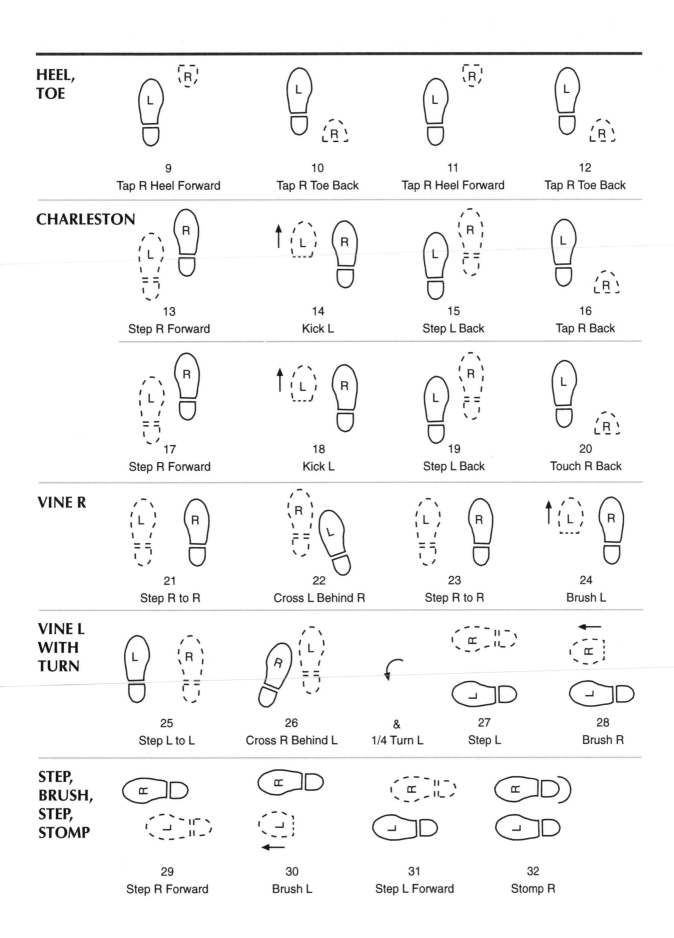

HEEL, TOE

9	10	11	12
Tap R Heel Forward	Tap R Toe Back	Tap R Heel Forward	Tap R Toe Back

CHARLESTON

13	14	15	16
Step R Forward	Kick L	Step L Back	Tap R Back

17	18	19	20
Step R Forward	Kick L	Step L Back	Touch R Back

VINE R

21	22	23	24
Step R to R	Cross L Behind R	Step R to R	Brush L

VINE L WITH TURN

25	26	&	27	28
Step L to L	Cross R Behind L	1/4 Turn L	Step L	Brush R

STEP, BRUSH, STEP, STOMP

29	30	31	32
Step R Forward	Brush L	Step L Forward	Stomp R

Coyote

This dance originated out of Canada. A great tempo for it is anywhere from 110 to 160 BPM.

Music Suggestions

"The Coyote and the Cowboy" by Ian Tyson

"I Sang Dixie" by Dwight Yoakam

"Neon Leon" by Sammy Kershaw

Step Descriptions

1-4   Walk forward R, L, tap R heel forward, hook R

5-8   Tap R heel forward, step R next to L, heel splits, feet together

9-12   Tap L heel forward, hook L, tap L heel forward, tap L foot back

13-16   Step L forward, kick R and clap hands, walk back R, L

17-20   Walk R back, tap L toe back, step L forward, tap R toe next to L

21-24   Touch R toe to R, touch R toe behind L, step R to R, touch L toe behind R

25-28   Grapevine L (step L to L, cross R behind L, step L to L), kick R and one-quarter turn L

29-32   Walk back R, L, stomp R next to L twice

Variations

1. On counts 15 to 18, replace the walk back with a rolling grapevine to the R.

2. On counts 25 to 28, do a rolling grapevine to the L and end with a one-quarter turn L and kick R (total one-and-one-quarter turn L).

Foot Map

FORWARD AND HOOK

1	2	3	4
Step R Forward	Step L Forward	Tap R Heel Forward	Hook R

HEELS

5	6	7	8
Tap R Heel Forward	Step R Next to L	Heel Splits	Together

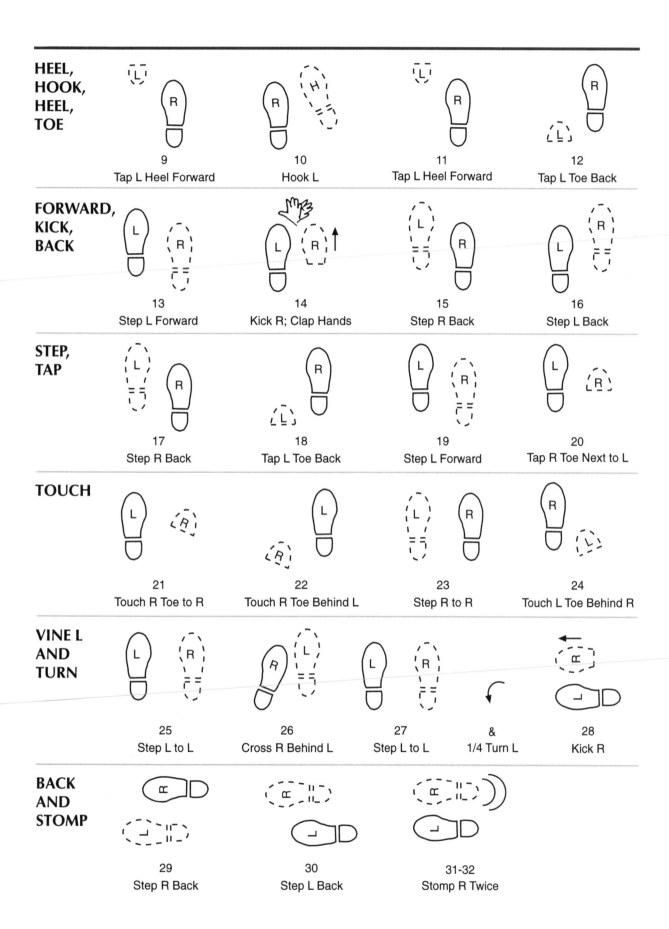

HEEL, HOOK, HEEL, TOE

9	10	11	12
Tap L Heel Forward	Hook L	Tap L Heel Forward	Tap L Toe Back

FORWARD, KICK, BACK

13	14	15	16
Step L Forward	Kick R; Clap Hands	Step R Back	Step L Back

STEP, TAP

17	18	19	20
Step R Back	Tap L Toe Back	Step L Forward	Tap R Toe Next to L

TOUCH

21	22	23	24
Touch R Toe to R	Touch R Toe Behind L	Step R to R	Touch L Toe Behind R

VINE L AND TURN

25	26	27	&	28
Step L to L	Cross R Behind L	Step L to L	1/4 Turn L	Kick R

BACK AND STOMP

29	30	31-32
Step R Back	Step L Back	Stomp R Twice

Down and Dirty

Also known as the Sleazy Slide, this dance is usually performed to cha-cha type music. During dance contests, contestants are allowed to demonstrate their own personal style of this dance and the wiggles can become quite suggestive. Perhaps we should rate this dance "R"!

Music Suggestions

"Friends in Low Places" by Garth Brooks

"Big Heart" by the Gibson Miller Band

"Why Haven't I Heard From You Lately?" by Reba McEntire

Step Descriptions

1-4   Step R to R, wiggle either hips or shoulders for two counts, bring L beside R while continuing to wiggle keeping weight on R

5-8   Step L to L, wiggle either hips or shoulders for two counts, bring R beside L while continuing to wiggle keeping weight on L

9-12   Repeat counts 5-8 (keep wiggling!)

13-16   Step R forward and rock hips forward, shift weight back to L and rock hips back, step R back and rock hips back, shift weight forward to L

17-20   Step R forward, pivot one-half turn L (end with weight on L), step R forward, pivot one-half turn L (end with weight on L)

21-24   Step R forward, one-quarter turn L (end with weight on L), stomp R and hold

Variations

1.   Begin the dance at step 13 instead of step 1. Continue the entire dance (after step 24 go to step 1).

2.   On counts 1 to 4, go to the L instead of to the R, and on counts 5 to 12, go to the R.

Foot Map

WIGGLE
TO R

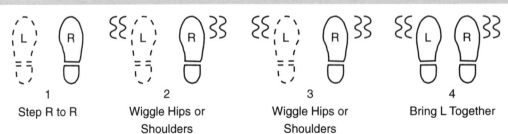

1	2	3	4
Step R to R	Wiggle Hips or Shoulders	Wiggle Hips or Shoulders	Bring L Together

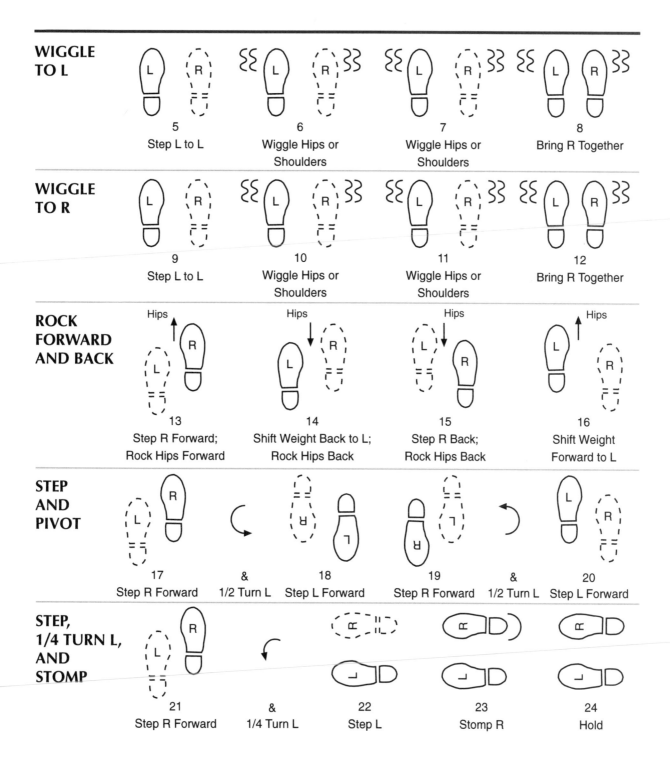

WIGGLE TO L

5	6	7	8
Step L to L	Wiggle Hips or Shoulders	Wiggle Hips or Shoulders	Bring R Together

WIGGLE TO R

9	10	11	12
Step L to L	Wiggle Hips or Shoulders	Wiggle Hips or Shoulders	Bring R Together

ROCK FORWARD AND BACK

13	14	15	16
Step R Forward; Rock Hips Forward	Shift Weight Back to L; Rock Hips Back	Step R Back; Rock Hips Back	Shift Weight Forward to L

STEP AND PIVOT

17	&	18	19	&	20
Step R Forward	1/2 Turn L	Step L Forward	Step R Forward	1/2 Turn L	Step L Forward

STEP, 1/4 TURN L, AND STOMP

21	&	22	23	24
Step R Forward	1/4 Turn L	Step L	Stomp R	Hold

Louie

This dance is similar to Slappin' Leather and is actually called by this name in some areas of the U.S. The Louie includes all the basic steps common to line dancing. For fun, try combining this dance with the Freeze.

Music Suggestions

"Honky Tonk Blues" by the Pirates of the Mississippi

"What Part of No" by Lorrie Morgan

"Some Girls Do" by Sawyer Brown

Step Descriptions

1-4   Tap R heel forward, step R next to L, tap L heel forward, step L next to R

5-8   Repeat counts 1-4

9-12   Tap R heel forward twice, tap R toe back twice

13-16   Tap R heel forward, tap R toe to side, tap R toe back, tap R toe to side

17-18   Slap R heel in front of body with L hand, one-quarter turn L, slap R heel in front of body with R hand (turning heel outward)

19-22   Grapevine R (step R to R, cross L behind R, step R to R), tap L

23-26   Grapevine L (step L to L, cross R behind L, step L to L), tap R

27-30   Walk back R, L, R, touch L

31-34   Step L forward, slide R together, step L forward, stomp R next to L ending with weight on both feet

35-38   Swivel L, return feet to center, swivel L, return feet to center

Variations

1. On counts 35 to 38, replace swivels with heel splits.

2. Replace slapping the foot with a tap of the foot on the floor.

Foot Map

HEELS

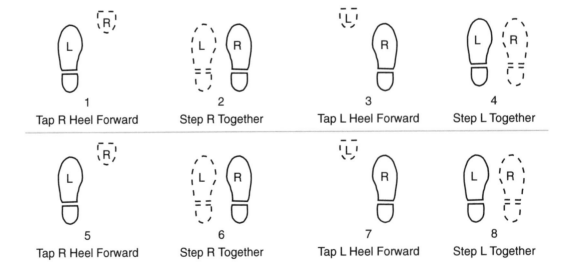

1	2	3	4
Tap R Heel Forward	Step R Together	Tap L Heel Forward	Step L Together

5	6	7	8
Tap R Heel Forward	Step R Together	Tap L Heel Forward	Step L Together

HEEL AND TOE

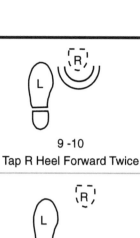

9 -10
Tap R Heel Forward Twice

11 - 12
Tap R Toe Back Twice

TOE TOUCHES

13
Tap R Heel Forward

14
Tap R Toe to Side

15
Tap R Toe Behind L

16
Tap R Toe to Side

SLAP AND TURN

17
Slap R Heel Front With L Hand

&
1/4 Turn L

18
Slap R Heel Front With R Hand

VINE R

19
Step R to R

20
Cross L Behind R

21
Step R to R

22
Tap L

VINE L

23
Step L to L

24
Cross R Behind L

25
Step L to L

26
Tap R

WALK BACK

27
Step R Back

28
Step L Back

29
Step R Back

30
Touch L

(continued)

Louie (continued)

FORWARD AND STOMP

31	32	33	34
Step L Forward	Slide R Together	Step L Forward	Stomp R to L

SWIVEL

35	36	37	38
Swivel L	Center	Swivel L	Center

Tap or Touch

Slappin' Leather

This dance is similar to the Louie. The name came about because you are going to slap your foot both at the end of the grapevines and in the "star" portion (instead of tapping your toes). Both young and old enjoy this dance.

Music Suggestions

"Reckless" by Alabama

"Honky Tonk Blues" by the Pirates of the Missisippi

"Ain't Goin' Down (Til the Sun Comes Up)" by Garth Brooks

"Born to Boogie" by Hank Williams, Jr.

Step Descriptions

1-4	Swivel R, bring feet to center, swivel L, bring feet to center
5-8	Repeat counts 1-4
9-12	Tap R to R, step R together, tap L to L, step L together
13-16	Repeat steps 9-12
17-20	Tap R heel forward twice, tap R toe back twice
21-22	Tap R heel forward, tap R toe to side
23-26	Slap R foot behind body with L hand, slap R foot behind body

with R hand turning R heel out, slap R foot in front of body with L hand and one-quarter turn L, slap R foot in front of body with R hand turning R heel out

27-30	Grapevine R (step R to R, cross L behind R, step R to R), tap L
31-34	Grapevine L (step L to L, cross R behind L, step L to L), and tap R
35-38	Walk back R, L, R, tap L next to R
39-42	Step L forward, step R together, step L forward, step R together and clap

Variations

1. On counts 1 to 8, replace swivels with heel splits.

2. On counts 23 to 26, replace slaps with taps on the floor.

3. On counts 30 and 34, slap foot instead of tapping.

4. On counts 38 and 42, stomp instead of tap.

Foot Map

SWIVEL

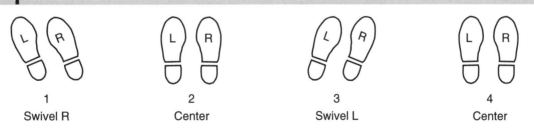

1	2	3	4
Swivel R	Center	Swivel L	Center

(continued)

Slappin' Leather (continued)

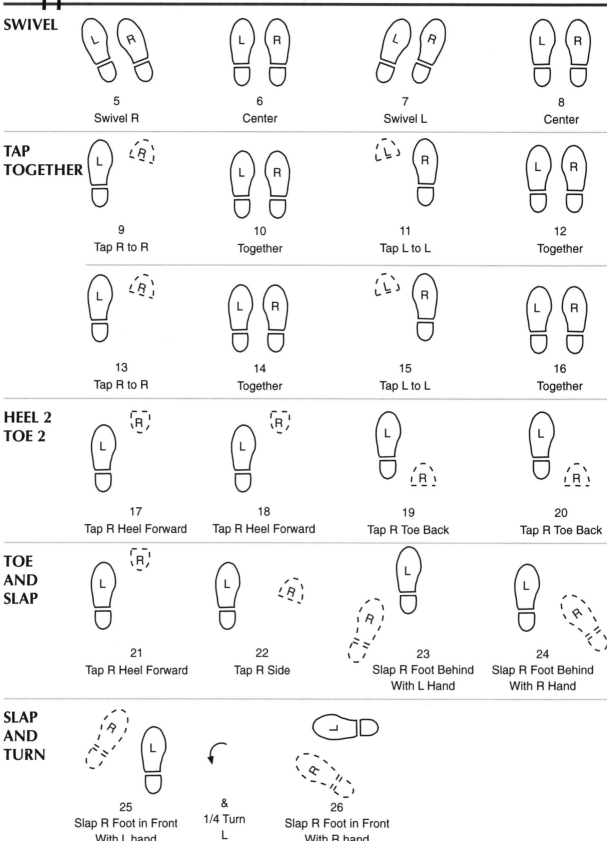

SWIVEL

5	6	7	8
Swivel R	Center	Swivel L	Center

TAP TOGETHER

9	10	11	12
Tap R to R	Together	Tap L to L	Together

13	14	15	16
Tap R to R	Together	Tap L to L	Together

HEEL 2 TOE 2

17	18	19	20
Tap R Heel Forward	Tap R Heel Forward	Tap R Toe Back	Tap R Toe Back

TOE AND SLAP

21	22	23	24
Tap R Heel Forward	Tap R Side	Slap R Foot Behind With L Hand	Slap R Foot Behind With R Hand

SLAP AND TURN

25	& 1/4 Turn L	26
Slap R Foot in Front With L hand		Slap R Foot in Front With R hand

VINE R

27	28	29	30
Step R to R	Cross L Behind R	Step R to R	Tap L

VINE L

31	32	33	34
Step L to L	Cross R Behind L	Step L to L	Tap R

WALK BACK

35	36	37	38
Step R Back	Step L Back	Step R Back	Tap L

WALK FORWARD

39	40	41	42
Step L Forward	Step R Together	Step L Forward	Together

One Step Forward, Two Steps Back

Four-Wall Dance
20 Counts

This dance was choreographed to fit a song called "One Step Forward" by the Desert Rose Band. My friend, Hillbilly Rick, says it should be called "One Step Forward, Two Steps Back, and Two Steps to the Side"!

Music Suggestions

"One Step Forward" by the Desert Rose Band

"Shut Up and Kiss Me" by Mary Chapin Carpenter

"I Wanna Go Too Far" by Trisha Yearwood

Step Descriptions

1-2	Step L forward, touch R next to L		11-12	Step R forward, touch L next to R
3-6	Step R back, step L next to R, step R back, touch L next to R		13-16	Step L back, step R next to L, step L back, touch R next to L
7-10	Step L to L, step R next to L, step L to L, touch R next to L		17-20	Step R to R, step L next to R, step R to R, one-quarter turn R and touch L

Variation

Any of the forward and backward movements can be performed to the diagonal. For example, when stepping forward on counts 1 and 2, step forward on L at a 45-degree angle to your left, then bring R behind L.

Foot Map

FORWARD

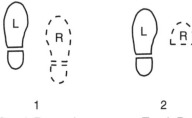

1	2
Step L Forward	Touch R

BACK

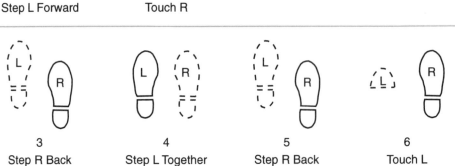

3	4	5	6
Step R Back	Step L Together	Step R Back	Touch L

STEP, TO-GETHER, STEP

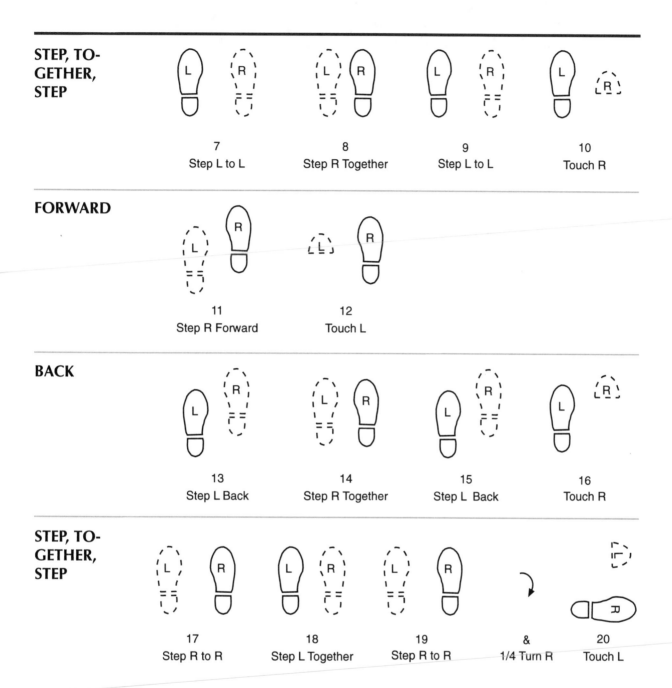

7	8	9	10
Step L to L	Step R Together	Step L to L	Touch R

FORWARD

11	12
Step R Forward	Touch L

BACK

13	14	15	16
Step L Back	Step R Together	Step L Back	Touch R

STEP, TO-GETHER, STEP

17	18	19	&	20
Step R to R	Step L Together	Step R to R	1/4 Turn R	Touch L

Electric Slide II

As the Electric Slide became popular, variations of it appeared. A different version of the dance was performed to funky songs and became known as the "New Electric Slide."

Music Suggestions

"Electric Slide" by Grandmaster Slice

"Funky Cowboy" by Ronnie McDowell

"Electric Slide" on *Christy Lane's Guide to Party Dances*

Step Descriptions

1-4   Tap R to R side, bring R foot to L, slide R, bring L foot to R

5-8   Tap L to L side, bring L foot to R, slide L, bring R foot to L

9-14   Tap R heel forward twice, tap R toe back twice, tap R heel forward, tap R toe back

15-16 Step forward R, kick L and at same time one-quarter turn R

17-20 Jazz box (cross L over R, step R back, step L to L, step R forward)

21-24 Jazz box (cross L over R, step R back, step L to L, jump ending with feet together)

Foot Map

TAP AND SLIDE

1	2	3	4
Tap R to Side	Together	Slide L to R	Bring L to R

5	6	7	8
Tap L to Side	Together	Slide R to L	Bring R to L

HEEL AND TOE

9, 10	11, 12	13	14
Tap R Heel Forward Twice	Tap R Toe Back Twice	Tap R Heel Forward	Tap R Toe Back

KICK, 1/4 TURN

15	16	&
Step R Forward	Kick L	1/4 Turn R

JAZZ BOX

17	18	19	20
Cross L Over R	Step R Back	Step L to L	Step R Forward

JAZZ BOX

21	22	23	24
Cross L Over R	Step R Back	Step L to L	Jump Together

 Slide

Tap L to side.

Slide L to R.

Flying Eight

This dance is a good opportunity to try a three-quarter turn. As you do the three-quarter turn, it will help if you think of a one-half turn and one-quarter turn together. Don't let the title fool you as this dance does not end on an eight count!

Music Suggestions

"Prop Me Up by the Jukebox" by Joe Diffie

"Fishin' in the Dark" by Nitty Gritty Dirt Band

"Walk Softly" by the Kentucky Headhunters

Step Descriptions

1-4   Grapevine L (step L to L, cross R behind L, step L to L), hop on L lifting R knee

5-8   Grapevine R (step R to R, cross L behind R, step R to R), hop on R and quarter turn R lifting L knee

9-12   Grapevine L (step L to L, cross R behind L, step L to L), three-quarter turn L on L landing on L lifting R knee

13-16   Walk forward R, L, R, hop on R lifting L knee

17-20   Step L forward, hop on L lifting R knee, step R forward, hop on R lifting L knee

Variation

This dance can be done with two lines facing each other (called "contra"). On counts 9 to 12, the partners pass by each other.

Foot Map

**VINE L
WITH
HOP**

1	2	3	4
Step L to L	Cross R Behind L	Step L to L	Hop L

**VINE R
WITH
HOP,
TURN**

5	6	7	&	8
Step R to R	Cross L Behind R	Step R to R	Hop R	1/4 Turn R

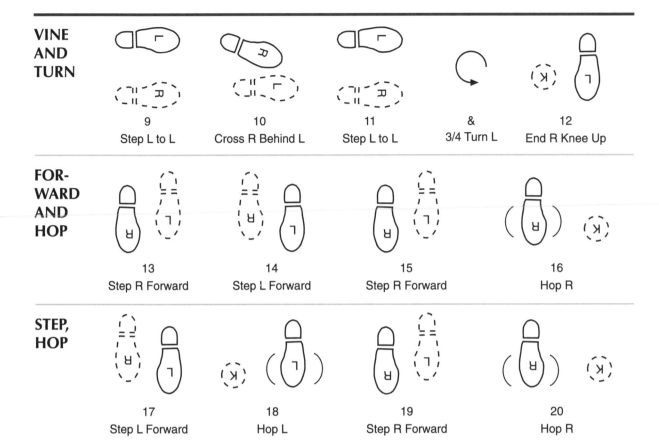

VINE AND TURN

9	10	11	&	12
Step L to L	Cross R Behind L	Step L to L	3/4 Turn L	End R Knee Up

FORWARD AND HOP

13	14	15	16
Step R Forward	Step L Forward	Step R Forward	Hop R

STEP, HOP

17	18	19	20
Step L Forward	Hop L	Step R Forward	Hop R

Grapevine

Step L to L.   Step R behind L.   Step L to L.   Tap R.

Reggae Cowboy

This is one dance for which you will not see many variations. Inspired by the song "Get Into the Reggae Cowboy" by the Bellamy Brothers, the tricky part of this dance is putting weight on your heel as you quarter-turn.

Music Suggestions

"Get Into the Reggae Cowboy" by the Bellamy Brothers

"Watch Me" by Lorrie Morgan

"Run for the Border" by Johnny Rodriquez

Step Descriptions

1&2	Shuffle forward R (step R forward, step L next to R, step R forward)
3&4	Shuffle forward L (step L forward, step R next to L, step L forward)
5&6	Repeat counts 1&2
7&8	Repeat counts 3&4
9-12	Jazz box R (step R forward, cross L over R, step back R, step L beside R)
13&14	Shuffle forward R (step R forward, step L next to R, step R forward)
15&16	Shuffle forward L (step L forward, step R next to L, step L forward)
17-20	Touch R heel forward, bring R to L, touch R toe to R, bring R to L
21-24	R heel forward putting weight on it as you make one-quarter turn L, step L, R heel forward putting weight on it as you make one-quarter turn L, step L

Foot Map

SHUFFLE

1	&	2	3	&	4
Step R Forward	Step L Together	Step R Forward	Step L Forward	Step R Together	Step L Forward

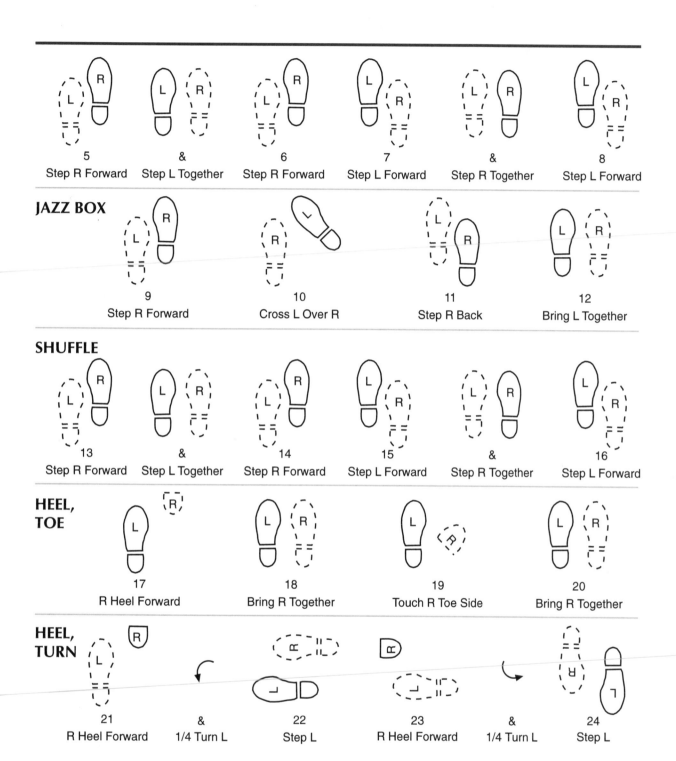

5	&	6	7	&	8
Step R Forward	Step L Together	Step R Forward	Step L Forward	Step R Together	Step L Forward

JAZZ BOX

9	10	11	12
Step R Forward	Cross L Over R	Step R Back	Bring L Together

SHUFFLE

13	&	14	15	&	16
Step R Forward	Step L Together	Step R Forward	Step L Forward	Step R Together	Step L Forward

HEEL, TOE

17	18	19	20
R Heel Forward	Bring R Together	Touch R Toe Side	Bring R Together

HEEL, TURN

21	&	22	23	&	24
R Heel Forward	1/4 Turn L	Step L	R Heel Forward	1/4 Turn L	Step L

Tennessee Twister

This is a perfect name for a dance that consists of swivels (and wiggles) with half-turns. After you learn this dance, try it to progressively faster music, such as "Looking Out for Number One" by Travis Tritt, and you will feel like a Tennessee Twister!

Music Suggestions

"I Ain't Got No Business" by Alabama

"Walk Softly" by the Kentucky Headhunters

"Little Miss Honky Tonk" by Brooks and Dunn

Step Descriptions

1-4	Swivel heels L and drop heels to ground twice, swivel heels R and drop heels to ground twice
5-8	Swivel heels L, then R, then L, then R
9-12	Tap R heel forward twice, tap R toe back twice
13-16	Step R forward, step L next to R, step R forward, step L next to R
17-20	Step R forward, scuff L and one-half turn R, step L forward, step R next to L

21-24	Step L forward, step R next to L, step L forward, scuff R and one-half turn L
25-28	Grapevine R (step R to R, cross L behind R, step R to R), scuff L and one-half turn R
29-32	Grapevine L (step L to L, cross R behind L, step L to L), stomp R ending with weight on both feet

Foot Map

HEEL DROPS

1-2
Swivel and Drop Heels L Twice

3-4
Swivel and Drop Heels R Twice

SWIVEL

5
Swivel L

6
Swivel R

7
Swivel L

8
Swivel R

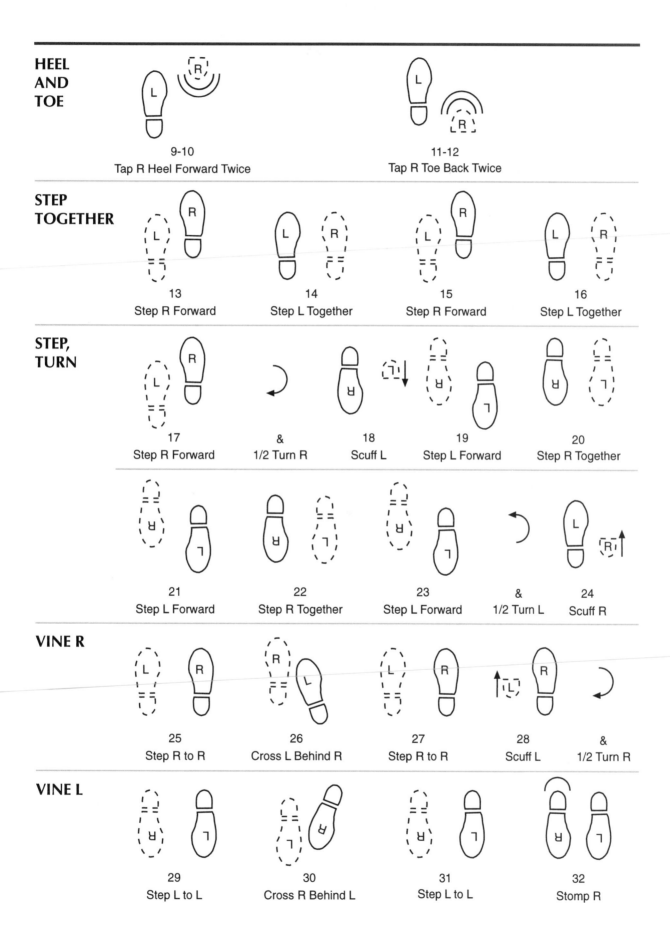

HEEL AND TOE

9-10
Tap R Heel Forward Twice

11-12
Tap R Toe Back Twice

STEP TOGETHER

13
Step R Forward

14
Step L Together

15
Step R Forward

16
Step L Together

STEP, TURN

17
Step R Forward

&
1/2 Turn R

18
Scuff L

19
Step L Forward

20
Step R Together

21
Step L Forward

22
Step R Together

23
Step L Forward

&
1/2 Turn L

24
Scuff R

VINE R

25
Step R to R

26
Cross L Behind R

27
Step R to R

28
Scuff L

&
1/2 Turn R

VINE L

29
Step L to L

30
Cross R Behind L

31
Step L to L

32
Stomp R

Cowboy Macarena

This dance, based on the famous Latin Macarena dance, is often performed on cruises. It is all hand movements except for the one-quarter turn. You can also shift your weight from right to left as you rock your hips side to side. The more creative you are at interpreting the dance, the better!

Music Suggestions

"Macarena" by Los Del Rios

"Macarena (Cowboy Version)" by Groovegrass Boyz

Step Descriptions

1	Touch hat with R hand	9	Blow smoke off R "gun"
2	Adjust hat in back with L hand	10	Blow smoke off L "gun"
3	Place R hand on L hip	11-12	Twirl both "guns"
4	Place L hand on R hip	13	Put "guns" back into holster
5	Draw R hand like a gun	14	Grab your horse's reins
6	Draw L hand like a gun	15-16	Ride away as you do one-quarter turn L
7-8	Shoot R "gun," shoot L "gun"		

Hitchhiker

This dance requires mostly upper-body movements and is great for kids and adults. Feel free to rock your hips side to side on each count to add some style.

Music Suggestions

"I Heard It Through the Grapevine" by Marvin Gaye

"Bop" by Dan Seals

"Get Into Reggae Cowboy" by the Bellamy Brothers

Step Descriptions

1-4	With R thumb, hitchhike twice to R side, with L thumb, hitchhike twice to L side	13-16	Roll fists around each other twice on L side, roll fists twice to front
5-8	With palm of R hand, wash window twice to R side, with palm of L hand, wash window twice to L side	17-20	Stand up and place R hand on L front hip, L hand on R front hip, R hand on R back hip, L hand on L back hip
9-12	Bend at waist and roll fists around each other twice on R side, roll fists twice to front	21-24	Hitchhike R thumb to R, hitchhike L thumb to L, jump one-quarter turn L, hold and clap

A Little Harder, But a Lot More Fun!

Intermediate Line Dances

Congratulations for making it this far! You should be proud of yourself. With your motivation you won't have any problem tackling more advanced dances. We're going to increase the tempo a bit and add some fancier footwork as you master combination steps like the cha-cha, shuffles, scoots, and slides performed together. The dances in this chapter may have the same number of counts as the beginning line dances, but there will be more steps than counts and also more turns. After you have learned one dance, try it with various types of music. Pick up the speed (tempo) of the music for a real challenge. Then try getting your brother or mother to do it with you. When you have some of these dances under your belt, read on to chapter 7, where you will learn some tricks about turning and be given pointers for style. This is where real enjoyment comes into play. Are you ready? We're going to have some fun now!

Alley Cat	125	Livin' La Vida Loca	137
Amos Moses	75	Night Fever	81
Black Velvet (Ski Bumpus)	104	Outlaw Waltz	92
Boot Scoot Boogie I	102	Power Jam	67
Copperhead Road	65	The Redneck	129
Country Strut	89	Rock Around the Clock	119
Cowboy Stomp	100	Six Step	95
Dance Ranch Romp	122	Southside Shuffle	71
Elvira	107	Thunderfoot	116
Funky Cowboy I	84	Tumbleweed	98
Funky Cowboy II	149	Tush Push	86
Ghostbusters	77	Waltz Across Texas	145
The Gilley	143	Watermelon Crawl	113
Honky Tonk Attitude	110	Wild Wild West I	73
Honky Tonk Stomp	69	Wild Wild West II	133
Hooked on Country	79		

Copperhead Road

This dance will give you a real feel of country dancing with the scoots, hitches, and stomps. It was inspired by the song "Copperhead Road" by Steve Earl. The dance is also known as the Kentucky Jug or Copperhead.

Music Suggestions

"Copperhead Road" by Steve Earle

"Oklahoma Swing" by Vince Gill

"Sticks and Stones" by Tracy Lawrence

Step Descriptions

1-4	Touch R heel forward, return R to center, touch L toe behind R, return L to center
5-8	Touch R toe behind L, step R to R, step L behind R, step R to R and one-quarter turn R
9-10	Hitch L and scoot sideways L twice on R foot
11-14	Grapevine L (step L to L, cross R behind L, step L to L), lift R behind L and slap R foot with L hand
15-18	Grapevine R (step R to R, cross L behind R, step R to R), lift L behind R and slap L foot with R hand
19-22	Walk back L, R, L, and scoot forward on L with R hitch
23-24	Stomp R forward, stomp L next to R ending with weight on R

Foot Map

HEEL TOGETHER, TOE TOGETHER

1	2	3	4
Tap R Heel Forward	Together	Tap L Behind R	Together

TAP BEHIND AND TURN

5	6	7	&	8
Tap R Behind L	Step R to R	Step L Behind	Step R to R	1/4 Turn R

(continued)

Copperhead Road (continued)

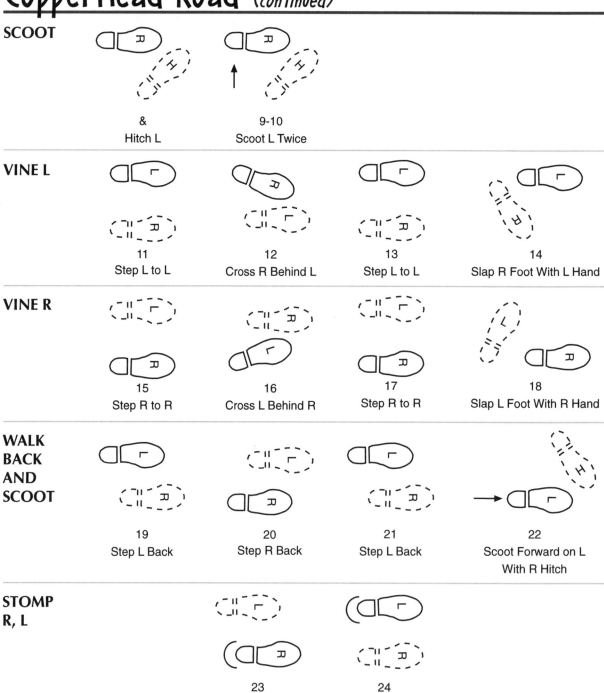

SCOOT

&
Hitch L

9-10
Scoot L Twice

VINE L

11
Step L to L

12
Cross R Behind L

13
Step L to L

14
Slap R Foot With L Hand

VINE R

15
Step R to R

16
Cross L Behind R

17
Step R to R

18
Slap L Foot With R Hand

WALK BACK AND SCOOT

19
Step L Back

20
Step R Back

21
Step L Back

22
Scoot Forward on L
With R Hitch

STOMP R, L

23
Stomp R Forward

24
Stomp L Together

Power Jam

Four-Wall Dance
24 Counts

One of the newest favored dances, this 24-count line dance can be performed to funky as well as country music.

Music Suggestions

"Gonna Make You Sweat" by C&C Music Factory

"Put Some Drive in Your Country" by Travis Tritt

"I Like It, I Love It" by Tim McGraw

Step Descriptions

1-4	Touch R toe to R, touch R together, step R to R, step L together
5-8	Touch L toe to L, touch L together, step L to L, step R together
9-12	Tap R heel forward twice, tap R toe back twice
13-16	Tap R heel forward, tap R toe back, tap R heel forward, tap R toe back

17&18	Shuffle forward R (step R forward, step L together, step R forward)
19&20	Shuffle forward L (step L forward, step R together, step L forward) with one-quarter turn R
21-24	Jazz box (cross R over L, step L back, step R back, hop feet together)

Foot Map

TOUCH R

1	2	3	4
Touch R Toe to R	Touch R Together	Step R to R	Step L Together

TOUCH L

5	6	7	8
Touch L Toe to L	Touch L Together	Step L to L	Step R Together

(continued)

Power Jam (continued)

HEEL 2,
TOE 2

9	10	11	12
Tap R Heel Forward	Tap R Heel Forward	Tap R Toe Back	Tap R Toe Back

HEEL,
TOE

13	14	15	16
Tap R Heel Forward	Tap R Toe Back	Tap R Heel Forward	Tap R Toe Back

SHUFFLE

17	&	18	19	&	20
Step R Forward	Step L Together	Step R Forward	Step L Forward	Step R Together; 1/8 Turn R	Step L Forward; 1/8 Turn R

JAZZ BOX

21	22	23	24
Cross R Over L	Step L Back	Step R to R	Hop Feet Together

Honky Tonk Stomp

Honky tonk songs and dances first appeared in many different places. This 32-count, two-wall dance originated in Arkansas and became one of the most widespread honky tonk dances. It is considered an intermediate-level dance because it is usually performed to a song 142 BPMs or faster.

Music Suggestions

"Honky Tonk Attitude" by Joe Diffie

"Honky Tonk Man" by Dwight Yoakam

"Hard Working Man" by Brooks and Dunn

Step Descriptions

1-4	Heel splits, together, heel splits, together	17-20	Grapevine R (step R to R, cross L behind R, step R to R), kick L
5-8	Tap R heel forward twice, tap R toe back twice	21-24	Grapevine L (step L to L, cross R behind L, step L to L), pivot turn L and kick R
9-12	Tap R heel forward, step R together, stomp L twice	25-28	Grapevine R (step R to R, cross L behind R, step R to R), kick L
13-16	Tap L heel forward, step L together, stomp R twice	29-32	Grapevine L (step L to L, cross R behind L, step L to L), stomp R ending with weight on both feet

Variation

Replace all grapevines with rolling grapevines.

Foot Map

HEEL SPLITS

1
Heel Splits

2
Together

3
Heel Splits

4
Together

HEEL 2, TOE 2

5
Tap R Heel Forward

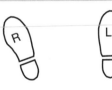
6
Tap R Heel Forward

7
Tap R Toe Back

8
Tap R Toe Back

(continued)

Honky Tonk Stomp (continued)

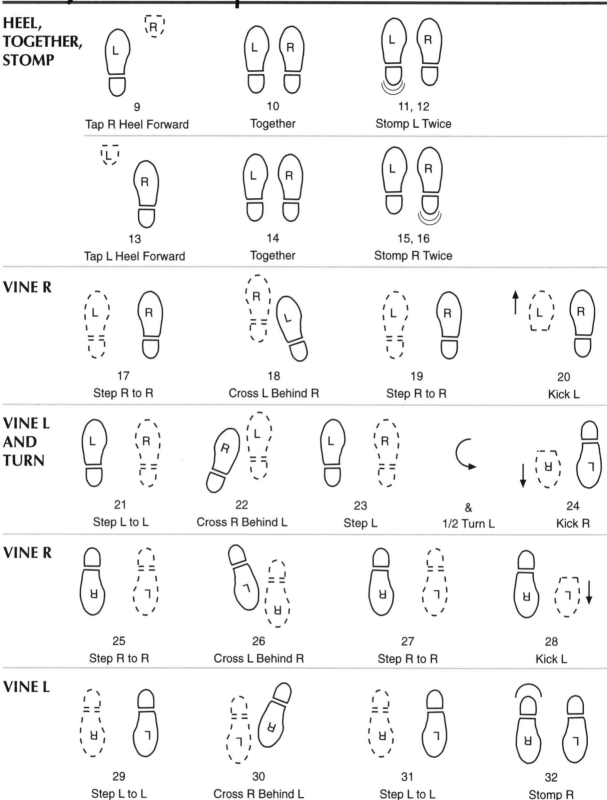

HEEL, TOGETHER, STOMP

9	10	11, 12
Tap R Heel Forward	Together	Stomp L Twice

13	14	15, 16
Tap L Heel Forward	Together	Stomp R Twice

VINE R

17	18	19	20
Step R to R	Cross L Behind R	Step R to R	Kick L

VINE L AND TURN

21	22	23	&	24
Step L to L	Cross R Behind L	Step L	1/2 Turn L	Kick R

VINE R

25	26	27	28
Step R to R	Cross L Behind R	Step R to R	Kick L

VINE L

29	30	31	32
Step L to L	Cross R Behind L	Step L to L	Stomp R

Southside Shuffle

In this dance, you will end up facing the opposite direction than you started. For variety, have your group form two lines facing each other. As you dance, cross between each other with right shoulders passing each other. Or, perform the dance in a circle instead of lines. Begin with four people in each circle and add more later.

Music Suggestions

"Mercury Blues" by Alan Jackson

"Hillbilly Rock" by Marty Stuart

"Big Ole' Truck" by Toby Keith

Step Descriptions

1-4	Swivel R, return heels center, swivel R, return heels center
5-8	Touch R heel forward twice, touch R toe back twice
9-12	Tap R heel forward, touch R toe back, touch R toe to R side, tap R behind L
13-16	Grapevine R (step R to R, cross L behind R, step R to R), scuff L
17-20	Grapevine L (step L to L, cross R behind L, step L to L), scuff R
21-24	Step R forward, drag L foot next to R, step R forward, one-half turn R and hitch L
25-28	Step L back, step R together, step L back, stomp R ending with weight on both feet

Variations

1. On counts 13 to 20, replace with rolling grapevines.

2. If in two lines, find a partner across from you and substitute counts 21 to 24 with the following: hook R elbows and perform one circle to the R and return to your original position.

Foot Map

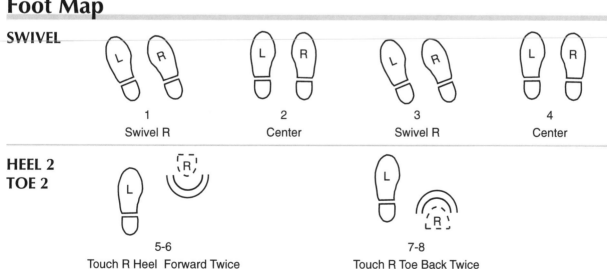

SWIVEL

1 — Swivel R
2 — Center
3 — Swivel R
4 — Center

HEEL 2 TOE 2

5-6 — Touch R Heel Forward Twice
7-8 — Touch R Toe Back Twice

(continued)

Southside Shuffle (continued)

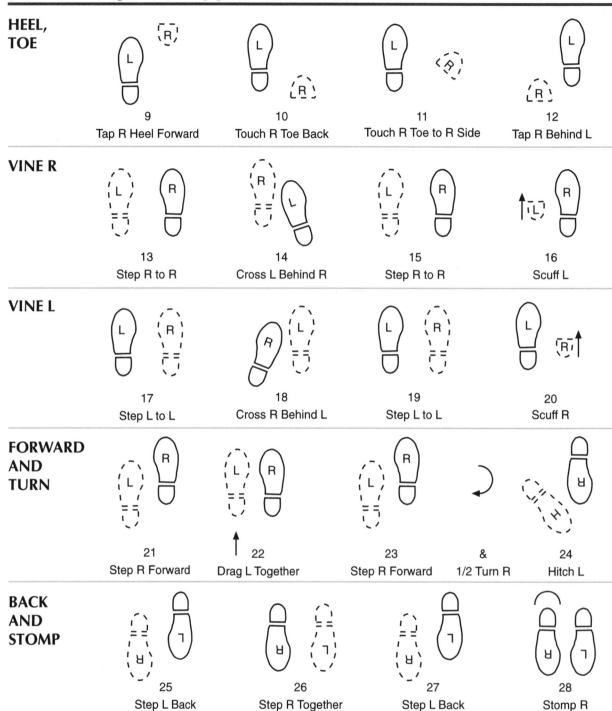

HEEL, TOE

9	10	11	12
Tap R Heel Forward	Touch R Toe Back	Touch R Toe to R Side	Tap R Behind L

VINE R

13	14	15	16
Step R to R	Cross L Behind R	Step R to R	Scuff L

VINE L

17	18	19	20
Step L to L	Cross R Behind L	Step L to L	Scuff R

FORWARD AND TURN

21	22	23	&	24
Step R Forward	Drag L Together	Step R Forward	1/2 Turn R	Hitch L

BACK AND STOMP

25	26	27	28
Step L Back	Step R Together	Step L Back	Stomp R

Wild Wild West I

This fun and lively dance consists of many shuffles. Keep your feet close to the floor almost like you are "skating" across the dance floor. After you master this dance, try taking as large steps as possible and travel across the floor to fast music. This will be loads of fun!

Music Suggestions

"Wild Wild West" by The Escape Club

"Brand New Man" by Brooks and Dunn

"God Bless Texas" by Little Texas

Step Descriptions

1-4   Lindy L (step L to L, step R beside L, step L to L, step on ball of R behind L, rock step forward on L)

5-8   Lindy R (step R to R, step L beside R, step R to R, step on ball of L behind R, rock step forward on R)

9-12   Triple-step forward L (step L forward, step R beside L, step L forward), pivot turn R and step ball of R behind L, step L forward

13-16   Triple-step forward R, pivot turn L and step ball of L behind R, step R forward

17-20   Walk forward L, R, L, stomp R ending with weight on L

21-24   Grapevine L (step L to L, cross R behind L, step L to L), one-half turn L and stomp R together putting weight on R

Variations

1. On counts 17 to 19, replace with a three-step turn forward.

2. On counts 21 to 23, replace with a rolling grapevine L.

Foot Map

LINDY L

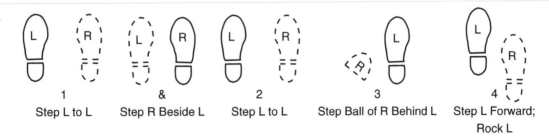

1	&	2	3	4
Step L to L	Step R Beside L	Step L to L	Step Ball of R Behind L	Step L Forward; Rock L

(continued)

Wild Wild West I (continued)

LINDY R

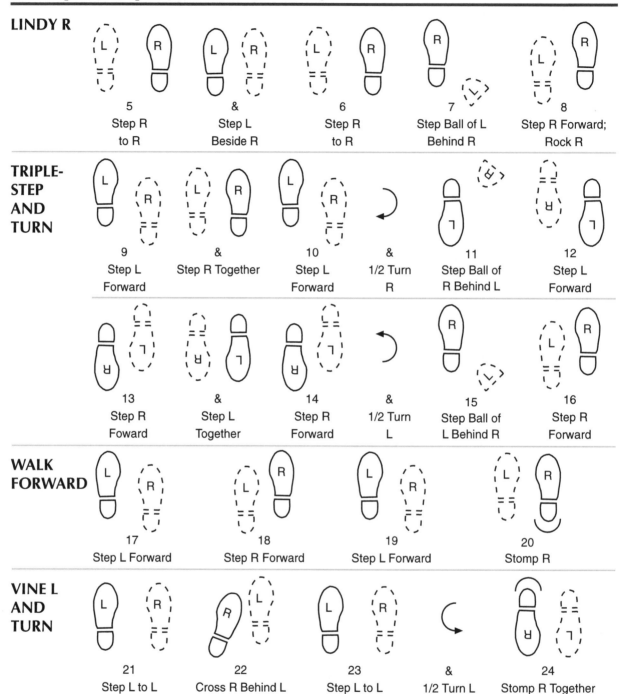

5	&	6	7	8
Step R to R	Step L Beside R	Step R to R	Step Ball of L Behind R	Step R Forward; Rock R

TRIPLE-STEP AND TURN

9	&	10	&	11	12
Step L Forward	Step R Together	Step L Forward	1/2 Turn R	Step Ball of R Behind L	Step L Forward

13	&	14	&	15	16
Step R Foward	Step L Together	Step R Forward	1/2 Turn L	Step Ball of L Behind R	Step R Forward

WALK FORWARD

17	18	19	20
Step L Forward	Step R Forward	Step L Forward	Stomp R

VINE L AND TURN

21	22	23	&	24
Step L to L	Cross R Behind L	Step L to L	1/2 Turn L	Stomp R Together

74

Amos Moses

The song "Amos Moses" by Jerry Reed will get your feet stomping on this dance! This almost qualifies as a beginning dance except for the ending—it's a little tricky!

Music Suggestions

"Amos Moses" by Jerry Reed

"Two of a Kind" by Garth Brooks

"A Good Run of Bad Luck" by Clint Black

Step Descriptions

1-4   Tap L heel forward, step L next to R, tap R heel forward, step R next to L

5-8   Heel splits, back together, heel splits, back together

9-12   Tap L toe to L side, tap L toe behind R, tap L toe to L side, step L next to R

13-16   Toe fan R, back together, toe fan R, back together

17-18   Toe fan R, back together

19&20   Shuffle forward L (step L forward, step R next to L, step L forward)

21&22   Shuffle forward R (step R forward, step L next to R, step R forward)

23&24   Repeat counts 19&20

25-26   Cross R over L and one-quarter turn L

27-30   Grapevine L (step L to L, cross R behind L, step L to L), stomp R ending with weight on R

Foot Map

HEEL, TOGETHER

1	2	3	4
Tap L Heel Forward	Together	Tap R Heel Forward	Together

HEEL SPLITS

5	6	7	8
Heel Splits	Together	Heel Splits	Together

TOE TAP

9	10	11	12
Tap L Toe Side	Tap L Behind R	Tap L Toe Side	Together

(continued)

Amos Moses *(continued)*

FAN R

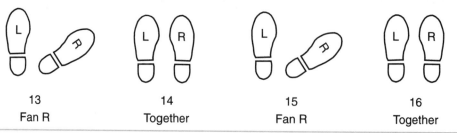

13	14	15	16
Fan R	Together	Fan R	Together

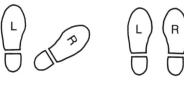

17	18
Fan R	Together

SHUFFLE L

19	&	20
Step L Forward	Step R Together	Step L Forward

SHUFFLE R

21	&	22
Step R Forward	Step L Together	Step R Forward

SHUFFLE AND TURN

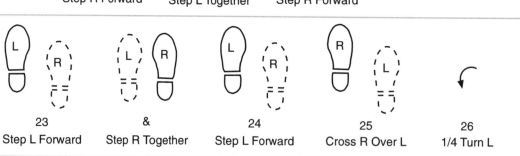

23	&	24	25	26
Step L Forward	Step R Together	Step L Forward	Cross R Over L	1/4 Turn L

VINE L

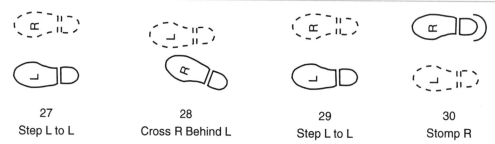

27	28	29	30
Step L to L	Cross R Behind L	Step L to L	Stomp R

Ghostbusters

This is a fun dance that originated in Florida. It can be performed with a funky style to the great song "Ghostbusters" as well as to country tunes.

Music Suggestions

"Ghostbusters" by Ray Parker, Jr.

"Indian Outlaw" by Tim McGraw

"Hooked on Country" by the Atlanta Pops

Step Descriptions

1-4	Walk forward R, L, R, kick L
5-8	Walk back L, R, L, ball change (cross ball of R behind L putting weight on it, step L in place)
9-12	Grapevine R (step R to R, step L behind R, step R to R), kick L
13-16	Grapevine L (step L to L, step R behind L, step L to L), stomp R
17-20	Tap R heel forward twice, tap R toe back, stomp R ending with weight on both feet
21-24	Swivel L, swivel R, scuff R and one-quarter turn L, high kick R
25-26	Shuffle back R (step R back, step L next to R, step R back)
27-28	Shuffle back L (step L back, step R next to L, step L back)

Variations

1. Add the following steps between counts 16 and 17 to make a 32 count dance: step R forward, hop on R foot, step L forward, hop on L foot.

2. On count 23 stomp instead of scuff before the high kick.

Foot Map

WALK AND KICK

1	2	3	4
Step R Forward	Step L Forward	Step R Forward	Kick L

WALK BACK, BALL CHANGE

5	6	7	&	8
Step L Back	Step R Back	Step L Back	Ball R Back	Step L in Place

(continued)

Ghostbusters (continued)

VINE R

9	10	11	12
Step R to R	Step L Behind R	Step R to R	Kick L

VINE L

13	14	15	16
Step L to L	Step R Behind L	Step L to L	Stomp R

HEELS

17	18	19	20
R Heel Forward	R Heel Forward	R Toe Back	Stomp R

SWIVEL AND TURN

21	22	23	&	24
Swivel L	Swivel R	Scuff R	1/4 Turn L	Kick R

SHUFFLE BACK

25	&	26
Step R Back	Step L Together	Step R Back

27	&	28
Step L Back	Step R Together	Step L Back

Hooked on Country

Hooked on Country is a popular line dance that originated in Florida. It will allow you to practice the well-liked shuffle-step, also known as the triple-step, which is used in many intermediate line dances.

Music Suggestions

"Just Hooked on Country" by the Atlanta Pops

"Ain't Nothin' Wrong With the Radio" by Aaron Tippin

"Sticks and Stones" by Tracy Lawrence

Step Descriptions

1&2	Shuffle back R (step R back, step L next to R, step R back)
3&4	Shuffle back L (step L back, step R next to L, step L back)
5-8	Walk forward R, L, R, kick L
9-12	Walk back L, R, L, step ball of R behind L and change weight to L
13-16	Grapevine R (step R to R, cross L behind R, step R to R), kick L

17-20	Grapevine L (step L to L, cross R behind L, step L to L), kick R
21-24	Step R to R, kick L, step L to L, kick R
25-28	Tap R heel forward twice, tap R toe back twice
29-32	Step R forward, one-quarter turn L and step L, stomp R, kick R

Variations

1. On counts 9 to 12, replace with walk back L, R, shuffle back L, R, L.

2. On counts 22 and 24, clap hands while performing kicks.

Foot Map

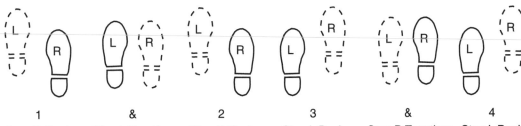

SHUFFLE BACK

1	&	2	3	&	4
Step R Back	Step L Together	Step R Back	Step L Back	Step R Together	Step L Back

WALK AND KICK

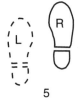

5	6	7	8
Step R Forward	Step L Forward	Step R Forward	Kick L

(continued)

Hooked on Country (continued)

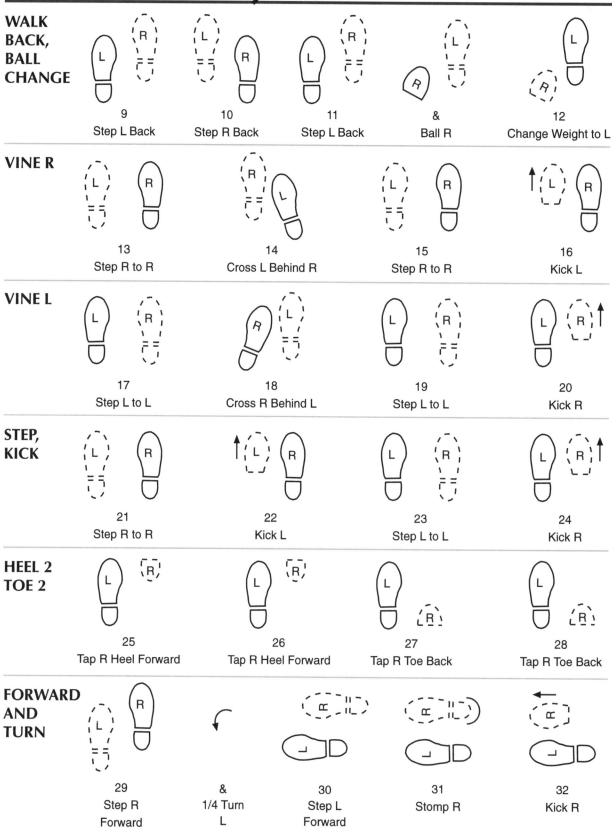

WALK BACK, BALL CHANGE

9	10	11	&	12
Step L Back	Step R Back	Step L Back	Ball R	Change Weight to L

VINE R

13	14	15	16
Step R to R	Cross L Behind R	Step R to R	Kick L

VINE L

17	18	19	20
Step L to L	Cross R Behind L	Step L to L	Kick R

STEP, KICK

21	22	23	24
Step R to R	Kick L	Step L to L	Kick R

HEEL 2 TOE 2

25	26	27	28
Tap R Heel Forward	Tap R Heel Forward	Tap R Toe Back	Tap R Toe Back

FORWARD AND TURN

29	&	30	31	32
Step R Forward	1/4 Turn L	Step L Forward	Stomp R	Kick R

Night Fever

This dance is also known as the "Stayin' Alive" line dance. Originated in the '70s, its popularity grew from the movie *Saturday Night Fever.*

Music Suggestions

"Stayin' Alive" by the Bee Gees

"The Hustle" by Van McCoy

"Le Freak" by Chic

Step Descriptions

1-4   Walk back R, L, R, tap L next to R and clap hands

5-8   Walk forward L, R, L, tap R next to L and clap hands

9-12   Step R to R, step L together, step R to R, tap L to L

13-16   Step L to L, step R together, step L to L, tap R to R

17&18   Kick ball change R (kick R, back on R ball, step L in place)

19&20   Repeat counts 17&18

21-24   Skate (twist the entire body) R, L, R, L

25-32   Step R with a small twist to R and point R index finger up straightening arm, step L with a small twist to L and small bend of knees, point R index finger across hips toward ground. Repeat 3 more times.

33-34   Roll fists in circle in front of body as hips bump L and R

35&36   Heel splits out, in, out, in (while continuing to roll fists)

37-40   Tap R heel forward, tap R toe back, tap R toe side, one-quarter turn L and kick R

Foot Map

WALK BACK

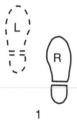

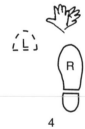

1	2	3	4
Step R Back	Step L Back	Step R Back	Tap L; Clap

WALK FORWARD

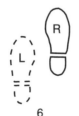

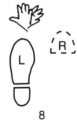

5	6	7	8
Step L Forward	Step R Forward	Step L Forward	Tap R; Clap

(continued)

Night Fever (continued)

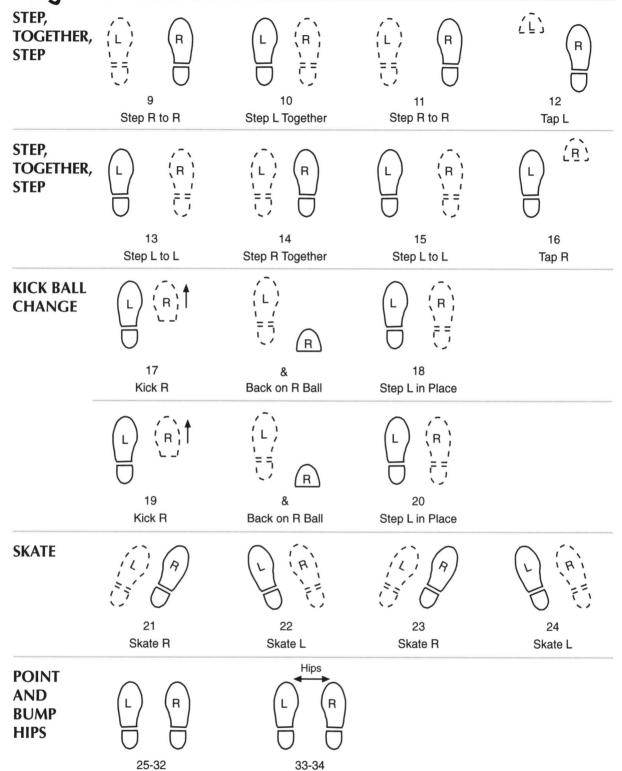

STEP, TOGETHER, STEP

9	10	11	12
Step R to R	Step L Together	Step R to R	Tap L

STEP, TOGETHER, STEP

13	14	15	16
Step L to L	Step R Together	Step L to L	Tap R

KICK BALL CHANGE

17	&	18
Kick R	Back on R Ball	Step L in Place

19	&	20
Kick R	Back on R Ball	Step L in Place

SKATE

21	22	23	24
Skate R	Skate L	Skate R	Skate L

POINT AND BUMP HIPS

Hips

25-32	33-34
Feet Center	Roll Fists in Circle
Disco Point — 4 Times	and Bump Hips Side to Side

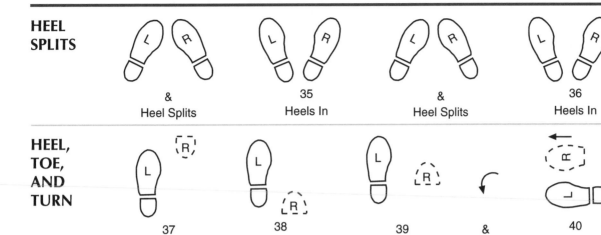

HEEL SPLITS							
& Heel Splits		35 Heels In		& Heel Splits		36 Heels In	

HEEL, TOE, AND TURN				
37 Tap R Heel Forward	38 Tap R Toe Back	39 Tap R Toe to Side	& 1/4 Turn L	40 Kick R

Heel Splits

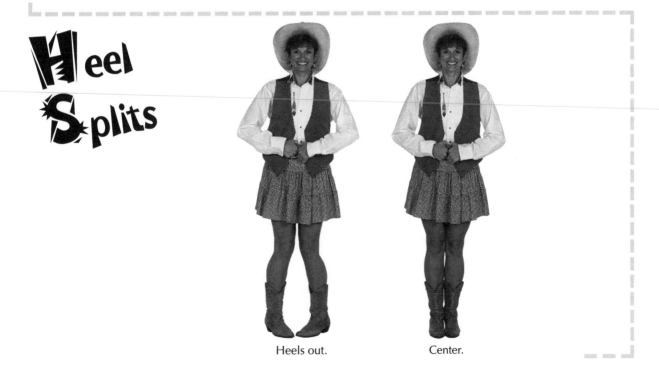

Heels out.   Center.

Funky Cowboy I

A line dance with a hip-hop flair, this dance can be performed to country music with a strong base beat or any funky-type music. What makes this dance special is putting your personal style into it.

Music Suggestions

"Funky Cowboy" by Ronnie McDowell

"Yippi Ti Yi Yo" by Ronnie McDowell

"Just Like New" by Wynonna Judd

Step Descriptions

1-4	Tap R toe to side, tap R toe behind L, tap R toe to side, tap R toe behind L
5-8	Grapevine R (step R to R, cross L behind R, step R to R), stomp L
9-12	Tap L toe to side, tap L toe behind R, tap L toe to side, tap L toe behind R
13-16	Grapevine L (step L to L, cross R behind L, step L to L), stomp R
17-20	Step R forward with knees bent, bounce R forward, rock back putting weight on L with knees bent, bounce backward
21-24	Rock forward putting weight on R, rock backward putting weight on L, rock forward again on R, rock back again on L
25&26	Shuffle forward R (step R forward, step L next to R, step R forward)
27&28	Shuffle forward L (step L forward, step R next to L, step L forward)
29-32	Step R forward and pivot turn L, step L back and pivot turn L, walk forward R, L

Foot Map

TAP R

1	2	3	4
Tap R to Side	Tap R Behind L	Tap R to Side	Tap R Behind L

VINE R

5	6	7	8
Step R to R	Cross L Behind R	Step R to R	Stomp L to R

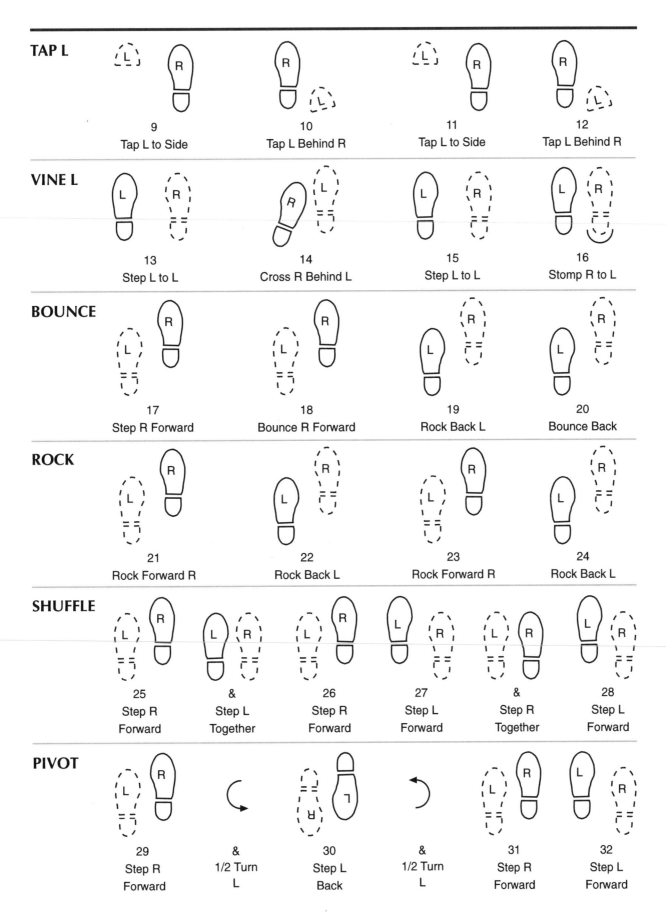

TAP L

9	10	11	12
Tap L to Side	Tap L Behind R	Tap L to Side	Tap L Behind R

VINE L

13	14	15	16
Step L to L	Cross R Behind L	Step L to L	Stomp R to L

BOUNCE

17	18	19	20
Step R Forward	Bounce R Forward	Rock Back L	Bounce Back

ROCK

21	22	23	24
Rock Forward R	Rock Back L	Rock Forward R	Rock Back L

SHUFFLE

25	&	26	27	&	28
Step R Forward	Step L Together	Step R Forward	Step L Forward	Step R Together	Step L Forward

PIVOT

29	&	30	&	31	32
Step R Forward	1/2 Turn L	Step L Back	1/2 Turn L	Step R Forward	Step L Forward

If you are going to learn line dancing, you have to know the Tush Push. From state to state, this is one dance that does not have many variations, and it rates in the top 10 line dances everyone should know. Originally this dance was choreographed to cha-cha music, so any type of music with a cha-cha beat can work. It's fun and energetic.

Music Suggestions

"Guitars and Cadillacs" by Dwight Yoakum

"God Bless Texas" by Little Texas

"Honky Tonk Crowd" by Rick Trevino

Step Descriptions

1-4	Tap R heel forward, bring R next to L, tap R heel forward twice
5-8	Switch feet and tap L heel forward, bring L next to R, tap L heel forward twice
9-12	Switch feet and tap R heel forward, switch feet and tap L heel forward, switch feet and tap R heel forward, hold and clap
13-16	Bump hips forward twice, bump hips back twice
17-20	Hip circles R twice
21-24	Cha-cha forward R (step R forward, step L together, step R forward, step L forward, step R back)
25-28	Cha-cha back L (step L back, step R together, step L back, step R back, step L forward)
29-32	Triple step R (forward R, step L forward, pivot turn R and step R forward)
33-36	Triple step L (forward L, step R forward, pivot turn L and step L forward)
37-40	Step R forward, one-quarter turn L and step L to L, step R next to L, stomp L ending with weight on R and clap

Variations

1. On counts 17 to 20, replace hip rolls with hip bumps forward, back, forward, back.

2. Try the Tush Push Kaleidoscope! Form two circles instead of lines, one in the inside facing out and one on the outside facing in.

Foot Map

R HEEL

1	2	3	4
R Heel Forward	Step R Together	R Heel Forward	R Heel Forward

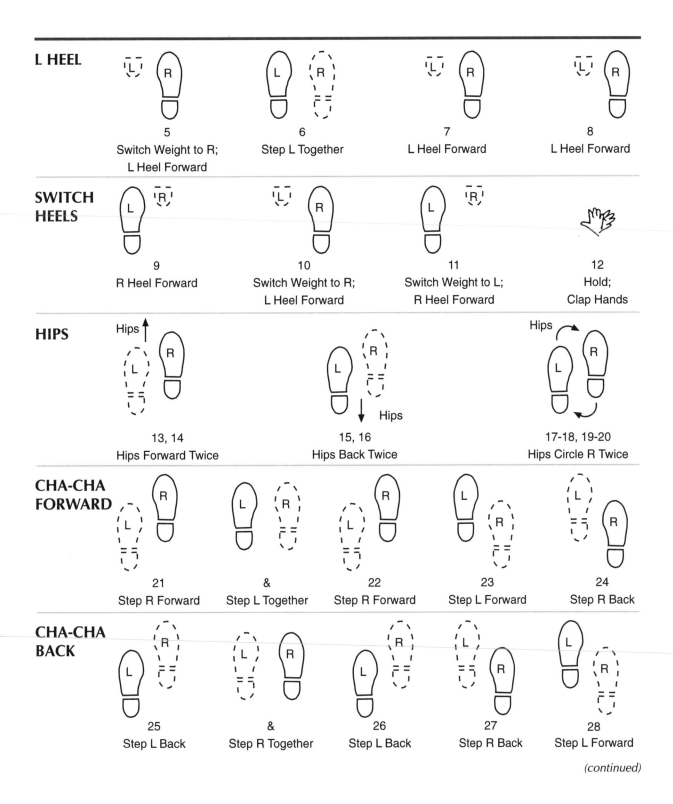

L HEEL

5	6	7	8
Switch Weight to R; L Heel Forward	Step L Together	L Heel Forward	L Heel Forward

SWITCH HEELS

9	10	11	12
R Heel Forward	Switch Weight to R; L Heel Forward	Switch Weight to L; R Heel Forward	Hold; Clap Hands

HIPS

Hips ↑   Hips ↓   Hips ↷

13, 14	15, 16	17-18, 19-20
Hips Forward Twice	Hips Back Twice	Hips Circle R Twice

CHA-CHA FORWARD

21	&	22	23	24
Step R Forward	Step L Together	Step R Forward	Step L Forward	Step R Back

CHA-CHA BACK

25	&	26	27	28
Step L Back	Step R Together	Step L Back	Step R Back	Step L Forward

(continued)

Tush Push *(continued)*

CHA-CHA WITH TURN

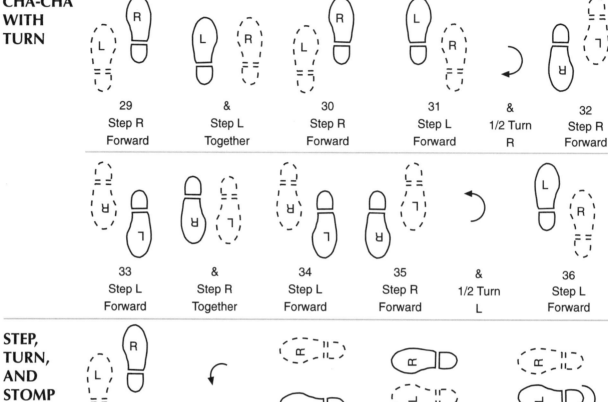

29	&	30	31	&	32
Step R Forward	Step L Together	Step R Forward	Step L Forward	1/2 Turn R	Step R Forward

33	&	34	35	&	36
Step L Forward	Step R Together	Step L Forward	Step R Forward	1/2 Turn L	Step L Forward

STEP, TURN, AND STOMP

37	&	38	39	40
Step R Forward	1/4 Turn L	Step L to L	Step R Next to L	Stomp L and Clap

Switch

R heel forward.   L heel forward.

88

Country Strut

This dance consists of struts (moving forward with a heel-toe action) and can be challenging when performed fast. Try strutting across the room continuously, and then gradually pick up speed. Have you ever tried tap dancing?

Music Suggestions

"God Bless Texas" by Little Texas

"I'm Only in It for Love" by John Coulee

"Redneck Riviera" by the Nitty Gritty Dirt Band

Step Descriptions

1-4   Tap R heel forward, hook R over L, tap R heel forward, tap R toe side

5-8   Tap R heel forward, step R next to L, tap L heel forward, hook L over R

9-12   Tap L heel forward, tap L toe to L side, tap L heel forward, tap L toe back

13-16   Charleston on L (step L forward, kick R, step R back, tap L toe back)

17-20   Step L to L, cross R behind L, pivot turn L and step L to L, scuff R

21-24   Strut forward (tap R heel forward, step R forward, tap L heel forward, step L forward)

25-28   Repeat counts 21-24

29-32   Cross R over L, one-quarter turn R and step L back, step R to R, step L forward

33-36   Jazz box (cross R over L, step L back, step R to R, step L together)

Foot Map

**HEEL,
HOOK**

1	2	3	4
Tap R Heel Forward	Hook R Over L	Tap R Heel Forward	Tap R Toe to R

(continued)

Country Strut (continued)

HEEL, TOGETHER, HEEL, HOOK

5	6	7	8
Tap R Heel Forward	Together	Tap L Heel Forward	Hook L Over R

HEEL, TOE

9	10	11	12
Tap L Heel Forward	Tap L Toe to L	Tap L Heel Forward	Tap L Toe Back

CHARLES-TON

13	14	15	16
Step L Forward	Kick R	Step R Back	Tap L Toe Back

VINE L, 1/2 TURN

17	18	&	19	20
Step L to L	Cross R Behind L	1/2 Turn L	Step L to L	Scuff R

STRUT

21	22	23	24
Tap R Heel Forward	Step R Forward	Tap L Heel Forward	Step L Forward

25	26	27	28
Tap R Heel Forward	Step R Forward	Tap L Heel Forward	Step L Forward

JAZZ BOX WITH TURN

29	&	30	31	32
Cross R Over L	1/4 Turn R	Step L Back	Step R to R	Step L Forward

JAZZ BOX

33	34	35	36
Cross R Over L	Step L Back	Step R to R	Together

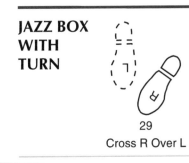

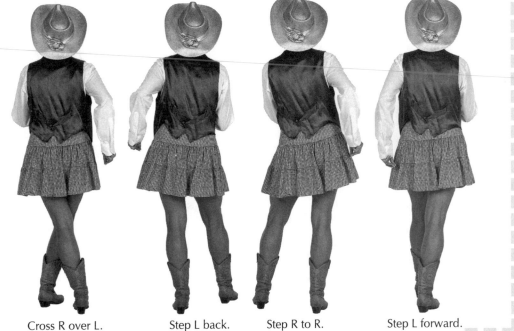

Cross R over L.　　　Step L back.　　　Step R to R.　　　Step L forward.

Outlaw Waltz

This dance can be performed to any waltz-type music with a "1-2-3" rhythm. Try dancing it smoothly by bending the knees and keeping the feet close to the floor. It can also be performed with a partner as a couples dance where both the man and woman dance the same footwork with their arms in the sweetheart position (see page 183).

Music Suggestions

"Could I Have This Dance" by Ann Murray

"Dream on Texas Ladies" by John Michael Montgomery

"Their Hearts Are Dancing" by the Forester Sisters

Step Descriptions

1-3   Tap R toe forward, tap R toe to R, cross R behind L

4-6   Step L forward, step R forward, brush L forward

7-9   Cross L in front of R, step R back, step L back

10-12   Cross R in front of L, rock back on L, step R together

13-15   Cross L in front of R, rock back on R, step L together

16-18   Cross R in front of L, rock back on L, step R to R and one-quarter turn R

19-21   Step L forward, step R together, step L in place

22-24   Step R back, step L back, step R next to L

25-27   Step L forward, step R next to L, step L in place

28-30   Three-step turn R

31-33   Cross L in front of R, rock back on R, step L next to R

34-36   Cross R in front of L, rock back on L, touch R next to L

Foot Map

TAP TOE

1 — Tap R Toe Forward

2 — Tap R Toe to R

3 — Cross R Behind L

WALK AND BRUSH

 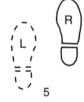

4 — Step L Forward

5 — Step R Forward

6 — Brush L Forward

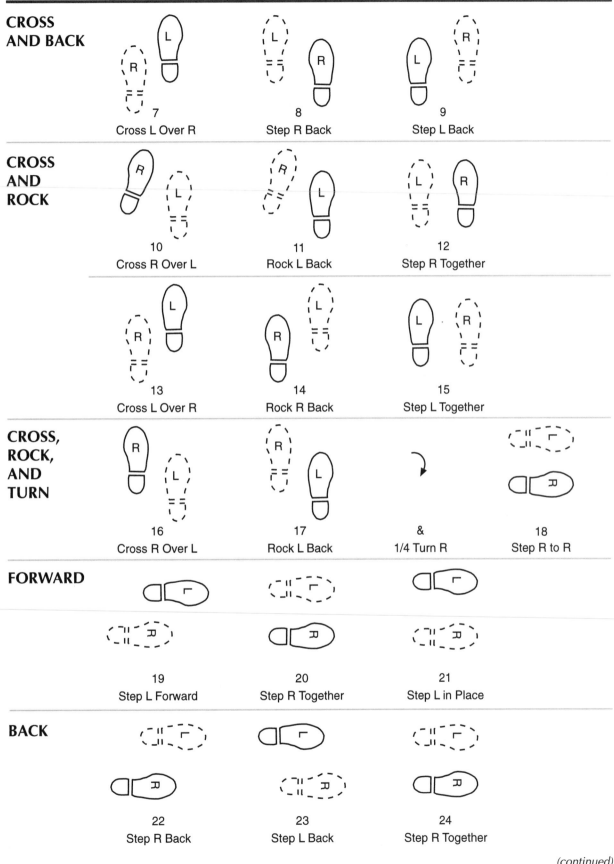

CROSS AND BACK

7	8	9
Cross L Over R	Step R Back	Step L Back

CROSS AND ROCK

10	11	12
Cross R Over L	Rock L Back	Step R Together

13	14	15
Cross L Over R	Rock R Back	Step L Together

CROSS, ROCK, AND TURN

16	17	&	18
Cross R Over L	Rock L Back	1/4 Turn R	Step R to R

FORWARD

19	20	21
Step L Forward	Step R Together	Step L in Place

BACK

22	23	24
Step R Back	Step L Back	Step R Together

(continued)

Outlaw Waltz (continued)

FORWARD

25	26	27
Step L Forward	Step R Next to L	Step L In Place

THREE-STEP TURN

28	&	29	&	30
Step R to R	1/2 Turn R	Step L	1/2 Turn R	Step R

CROSS AND ROCK

31	32	33
Cross L Over R	Rock R Back	Step L Together

CROSS AND ROCK

34	35	36
Cross R Over L	Rock L Back	Touch R Together

Six Step

Balance will help you perform this dance. Practice standing on one foot and bringing your other foot in a hook position, and hold it for five seconds while standing tall.

Music Suggestions

"Two of a Kind" by Garth Brooks

"My Maria" by Brooks and Dunn

"I Feel Lucky" by Mary Chapin Carpenter

Step Descriptions

1-4	Split heels apart and together twice
5-8	Tap R heel forward twice, tap R toe back twice
9-12	Tap R heel forward, tap R toe back, tap R heel forward, hook R over L
13-16	Tap R heel forward, step R next to L, fan out and in
17-20	Tap L heel forward twice, tap L toe back twice
21-24	Tap L heel forward, tap L toe back, tap L heel forward, hook L over R

25-28	Tap L heel forward, step L next to R, fan R toe out and together, fan L toe out and together
29-32	Step L forward, chug with R knee up, step R forward, pivot turn L bringing L knee up
33-36	Step L forward, kick R to side, cross R behind L, step L next to R
37-40	Scuff R, jump to R side and land R, step L next to R, scuff R
41-42	Jump to R side and land R, step L next to R

Foot Map

HEEL SPLITS

1	2	3	4
Heel Splits	Together	Heel Splits	Together

HEEL 2, TOE 2

5, 6	7, 8
Tap R Heel Forward Twice	Tap R Toe Back Twice

(continued)

Six Step (continued)

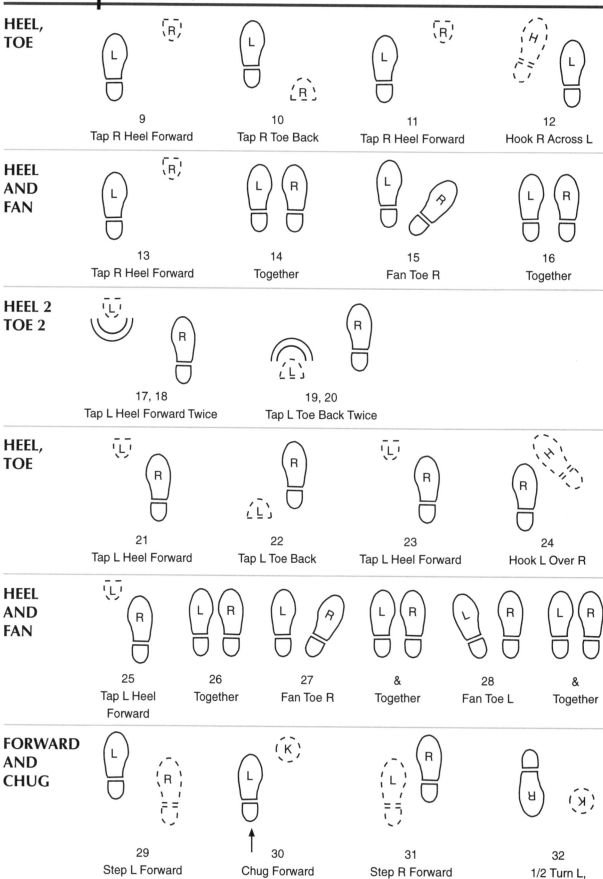

HEEL, TOE

9	10	11	12
Tap R Heel Forward	Tap R Toe Back	Tap R Heel Forward	Hook R Across L

HEEL AND FAN

13	14	15	16
Tap R Heel Forward	Together	Fan Toe R	Together

HEEL 2 TOE 2

17, 18	19, 20
Tap L Heel Forward Twice	Tap L Toe Back Twice

HEEL, TOE

21	22	23	24
Tap L Heel Forward	Tap L Toe Back	Tap L Heel Forward	Hook L Over R

HEEL AND FAN

25	26	27	&	28	&
Tap L Heel Forward	Together	Fan Toe R	Together	Fan Toe L	Together

FORWARD AND CHUG

29	30	31	32
Step L Forward	Chug Forward	Step R Forward	1/2 Turn L, L Knee Up

**STEP,
KICK**

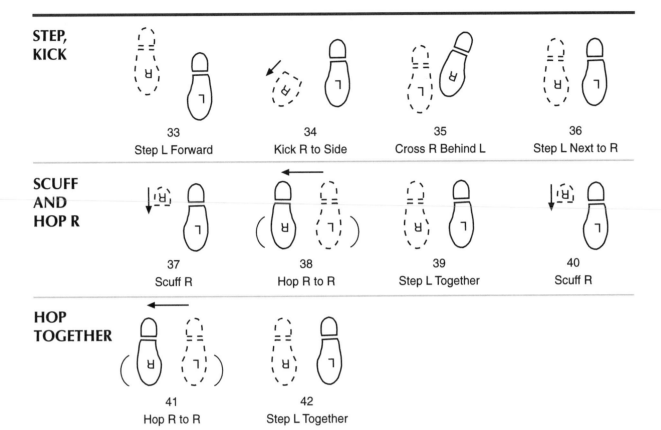

33	34	35	36
Step L Forward	Kick R to Side	Cross R Behind L	Step L Next to R

**SCUFF
AND
HOP R**

37	38	39	40
Scuff R	Hop R to R	Step L Together	Scuff R

**HOP
TOGETHER**

41	42
Hop R to R	Step L Together

Chug

Tumbleweed

There are six different Tumbleweed line dances that are popular throughout the United States. This version was selected based on a national survey of teachers.

Music Suggestions

"Thank God for You" by Sawyer Brown

"Rockin' With the Rhythm" by The Judds

"Hey Baby" by Marty Stuart

Step Descriptions

1-4   Kick R forward and step R back, walk back L, R, tap L toe back

5&6   Shuffle forward L (step L forward, step R together, step L forward)

7&8   Shuffle forward R (step R forward, step L together, step R forward)

9-10   Step L forward, pivot turn R and step R forward

11&12 Shuffle forward L (step L forward, step R together, step L forward)

13-16   Step R forward, one-quarter turn L and step L forward, step R forward, one-quarter turn L and step L forward

17-20   Cross R over L, step L to L, cross R behind L, spiral turn R and keep weight on R ending with feet together

21-24   Cross L over R, step together, swivel heels R, bring heels to center

Foot Map

KICK, BACK

1	&	2	3	4
Kick R Forward	Step R Back	Step L Back	Step R Back	Tap L Back

SHUFFLE

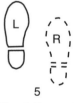  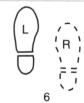

5	&	6
Step L Forward	Step R Together	Step L Forward

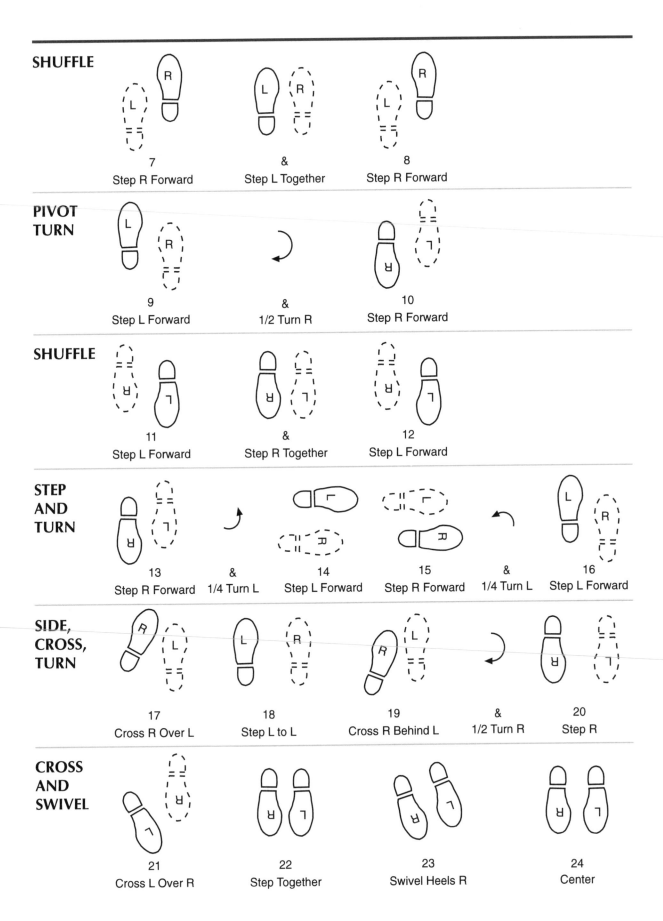

SHUFFLE

7	&	8
Step R Forward	Step L Together	Step R Forward

PIVOT TURN

9	&	10
Step L Forward	1/2 Turn R	Step R Forward

SHUFFLE

11	&	12
Step L Forward	Step R Together	Step L Forward

STEP AND TURN

13	&	14	15	&	16
Step R Forward	1/4 Turn L	Step L Forward	Step R Forward	1/4 Turn L	Step L Forward

SIDE, CROSS, TURN

17	18	19	&	20
Cross R Over L	Step L to L	Cross R Behind L	1/2 Turn R	Step R

CROSS AND SWIVEL

21	22	23	24
Cross L Over R	Step Together	Swivel Heels R	Center

Cowboy Stomp

This dance was choreographed to the song "The Cowboy Stomp" by Curtis Day. Originating in New York, the stomps give the dance its personality.

Music Suggestion

"The Cowboy Stomp" by Curtis Day

Step Descriptions

1-4   Swivel heels R, swivel toes R, swivel heels R, swivel toes R (while traveling R)

5-8   Touch R toe to side, pivot turn R, step R next to L, touch L toe to L side, step L next to R

9-12   Stomp R, kick L forward, kick L to L side, stomp L

13-16   Stomp R forward, kick L forward, kick L to L side, stomp L

17-20   Stomp R forward, step L forward, pivot turn R, step R forward, stomp L

21-24   Stomp R forward, step L forward, pivot turn R, step R to R, stomp L forward

25-28   Stomp R forward, brush L out, brush L in and hook, brush L out

29-32   Step L to L, step R behind L, one-quarter turn L and step L to L, stomp R ending with weight even on both feet

Foot Map

SWIVEL AND TRAVEL R

1	2	3	4
Swivel Heels R	Swivel Toes R	Swivel Heels R	Swivel Toes R

TOUCH AND TURN

5	&	6	7	8
Touch R Toe to Side	1/2 Turn R	Step R Together	Touch L Toe to Side	Step L Together

STOMP AND KICK

9	10	11	12
Stomp R	Kick L	Kick L to Side	Stomp L

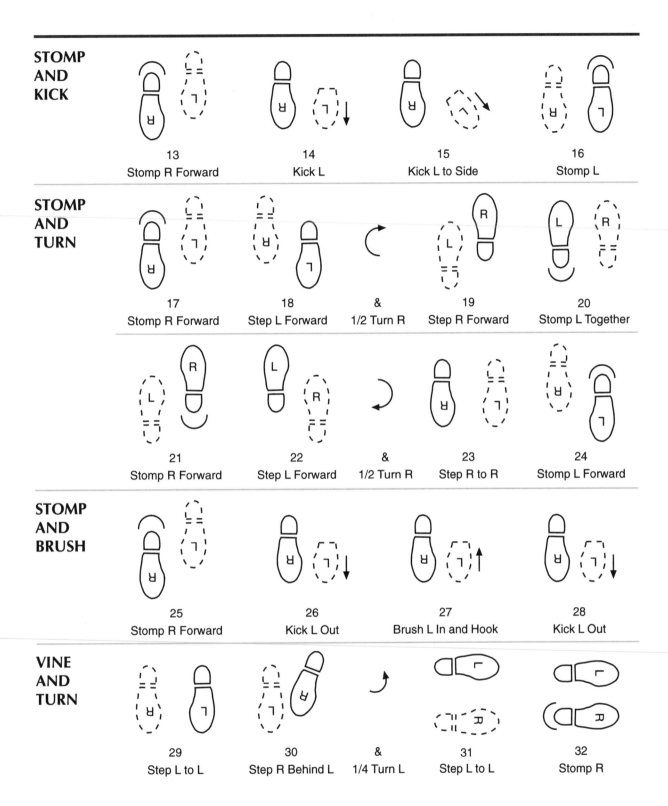

STOMP AND KICK

13	14	15	16
Stomp R Forward	Kick L	Kick L to Side	Stomp L

STOMP AND TURN

17	18	&	19	20
Stomp R Forward	Step L Forward	1/2 Turn R	Step R Forward	Stomp L Together

21	22	&	23	24
Stomp R Forward	Step L Forward	1/2 Turn R	Step R to R	Stomp L Forward

STOMP AND BRUSH

25	26	27	28
Stomp R Forward	Kick L Out	Brush L In and Hook	Kick L Out

VINE AND TURN

29	30	&	31	32
Step L to L	Step R Behind L	1/4 Turn L	Step L to L	Stomp R

Boot Scoot Boogie 1

There are numerous regional variations for this dance. This is one of the versions that has been seen performed at many dance clubs around the United States.

Music Suggestions

"Boot Scootin' Boogie" by Brooks and Dunn

"When She Cries" by Restless Heart

"Lost and Found" by Brooks and Dunn

Step Descriptions

1-4　Step L forward, pivot turn R and step R forward, step L forward, pivot turn R and step R forward

5-8　Grapevine L (step L to L, cross R behind L, step L to L), stomp R and clap

9-12　Step R forward, pivot turn L and step L forward, step R forward, pivot turn L and step L forward

13-16　Grapevine R (step R to R, cross L behind R, step R to R), stomp L and clap

17-20　Touch L heel forward, hook L in front of R, step L forward, scoot R next to L

21-24　Step L forward (bend knees and push L hip up and forward), pivot turn R and step R forward, pivot turn L (bend knees and push R hip up and forward), and step R forward

25-28　Step L forward, one-quarter turn L and hitch R, cross R over L, hold and clap

Foot Map

PIVOT TURN

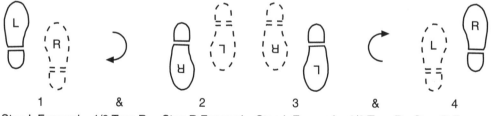

1	&	2	3	&	4
Step L Forward	1/2 Turn R	Step R Forward	Step L Forward	1/2 Turn R	Step R Forward

VINE L

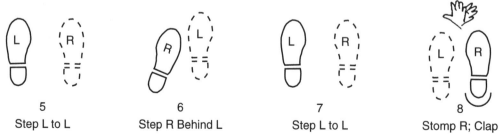

5	6	7	8
Step L to L	Step R Behind L	Step L to L	Stomp R; Clap

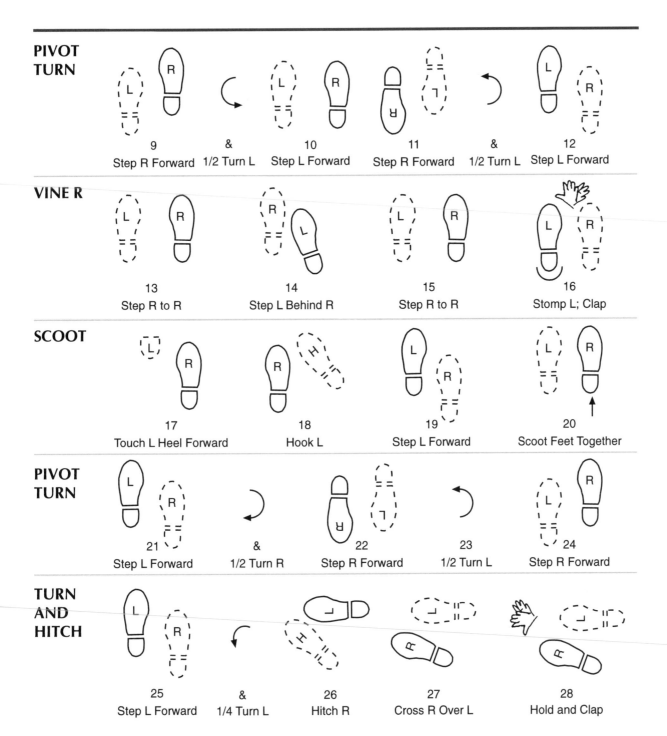

PIVOT TURN

9	&	10	11	&	12
Step R Forward	1/2 Turn L	Step L Forward	Step R Forward	1/2 Turn L	Step L Forward

VINE R

13	14	15	16
Step R to R	Step L Behind R	Step R to R	Stomp L; Clap

SCOOT

17	18	19	20
Touch L Heel Forward	Hook L	Step L Forward	Scoot Feet Together

PIVOT TURN

21	&	22	23	24
Step L Forward	1/2 Turn R	Step R Forward	1/2 Turn L	Step R Forward

TURN AND HITCH

25	&	26	27	28
Step L Forward	1/4 Turn L	Hitch R	Cross R Over L	Hold and Clap

Black Velvet (Ski Bumpus)

The Black Velvet and Ski Bumpus are the same dance. It just depends on which part of the United States you live in as to which name you call it. This is one dance that has remained popular with very few variations since its origin.

Music Suggestions

"Black Velvet" by Alannah Myles

"Ski Bumpus" by Wickline Band

"Be My Baby Tonight" by John Michael Montgomery

Step Descriptions

1&2	Shuffle forward R (step R forward, step L together, step R forward)
3&4	Shuffle forward L (step L forward, step R together, step L forward)
5-6	Step R forward, pivot turn L and step L forward
7-10	Shuffle forward R, shuffle forward L
11-12	Step R forward, pivot turn L and step L forward
13-16	Jazz box L (cross R over L, step L back, step R to R, stomp L together)
17-20	Repeat counts 13-16

21-24	Tap R toe to R side, step R next to L, tap L toe to L side, step L next to R
25-28	Repeat counts 21-24
29-32	Kick ball change R twice (kick R, step back on the ball of R, step L in place)
33-34	Step R forward, pivot turn L and step L forward
35-38	Repeat counts 29-32
39-40	Repeat counts 33-34

Variation

This dance can be performed as a "contra" line dance with partners facing each other. The lines will pass through each other on steps 1 to 4 and 7 to 10.

Foot Map

SHUFFLE

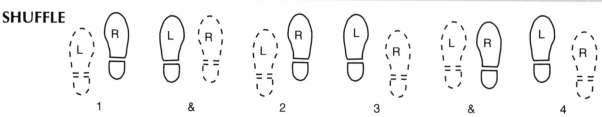

1	&	2	3	&	4
Step R Forward	Step L Together	Step R Forward	Step L Forward	Step R Together	Step L Forward

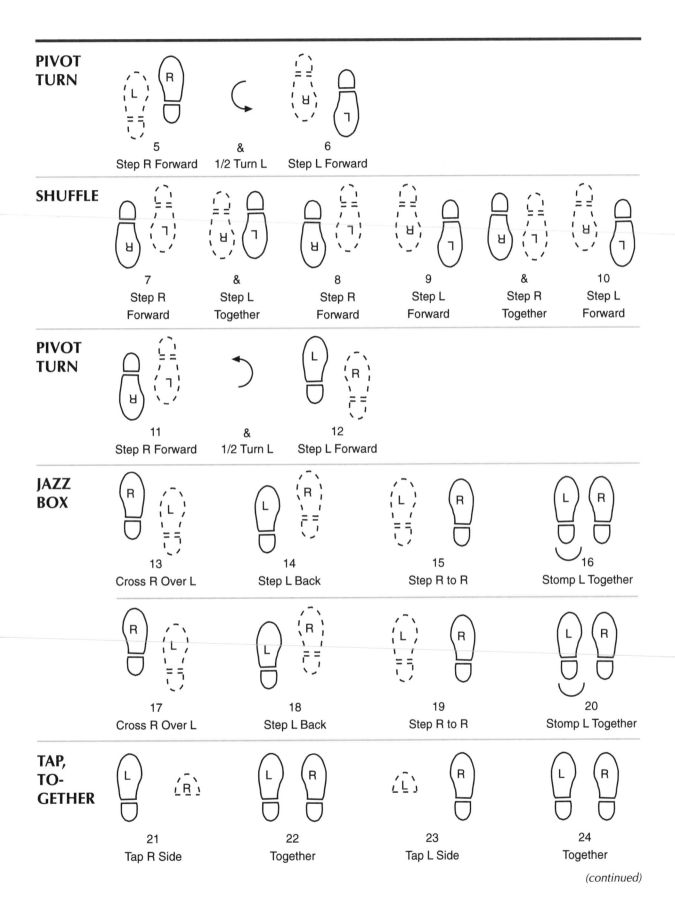

PIVOT TURN

5	&	6
Step R Forward	1/2 Turn L	Step L Forward

SHUFFLE

7	&	8	9	&	10
Step R Forward	Step L Together	Step R Forward	Step L Forward	Step R Together	Step L Forward

PIVOT TURN

11	&	12
Step R Forward	1/2 Turn L	Step L Forward

JAZZ BOX

13	14	15	16
Cross R Over L	Step L Back	Step R to R	Stomp L Together

17	18	19	20
Cross R Over L	Step L Back	Step R to R	Stomp L Together

TAP, TO-GETHER

21	22	23	24
Tap R Side	Together	Tap L Side	Together

(continued)

Black Velvet (Ski Bumpus) *(continued)*

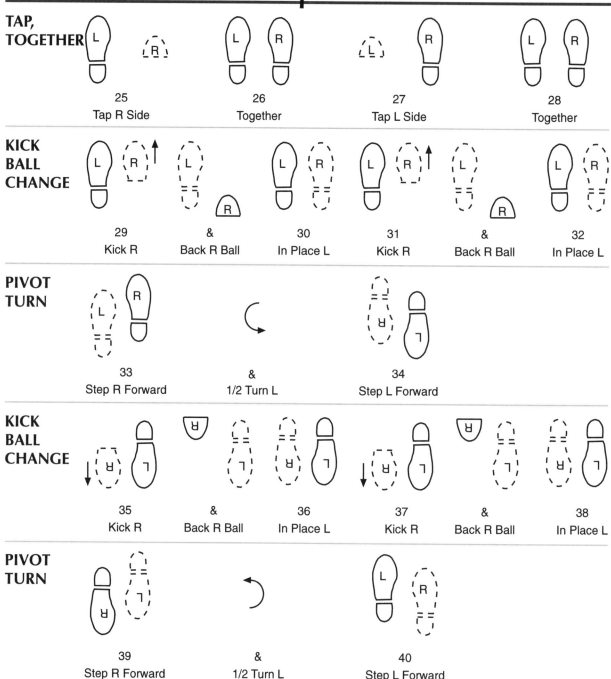

TAP, TOGETHER

25	26	27	28
Tap R Side	Together	Tap L Side	Together

KICK BALL CHANGE

29	&	30	31	&	32
Kick R	Back R Ball	In Place L	Kick R	Back R Ball	In Place L

PIVOT TURN

33	&	34
Step R Forward	1/2 Turn L	Step L Forward

KICK BALL CHANGE

35	&	36	37	&	38
Kick R	Back R Ball	In Place L	Kick R	Back R Ball	In Place L

PIVOT TURN

39	&	40
Step R Forward	1/2 Turn L	Step L Forward

Elvira

The name "Elvira" has been given to many dances. However, this is the most popular version as of the writing of this book. Of course, the hit song "Elvira" by the Oak Ridge Boys is what really made this dance popular. Even though you will face just one wall, get ready for lots of turns and triple steps!

Music Suggestions

"Elvira" by the Oak Ridge Boys

"Have Mercy" by The Judds

"Should Have Asked Her Faster" by Ricky Van Shelton

Step Descriptions

1-4   Lindy R (step R to R, step L to R, step R to R, ball change L behind R, step R)

5-8   Lindy L (repeat 1-4 using opposite feet to the left)

9-12   Triple-step forward (step R forward, step L next to R, step R forward), step L forward, pivot turn R and step R

13-16   Triple-step forward (step L forward, step R next to L, step L forward), step R forward, one-quarter turn L and step L

17-20   Step R forward, pivot turn L and step L, triple-step forward R (R, L, R)

21-24   Step L forward, pivot turn R and step R, triple-step forward L (L, R, L)

25-28   One-quarter turn L and walk forward R, L, R, kick L and clap

29-32   Walk back L, R, L, stomp R

Variations

1. Eliminate steps 21 to 24.

2. Replace count 32 with a ball change (R, L) for the ending.

Foot Map

LINDY R

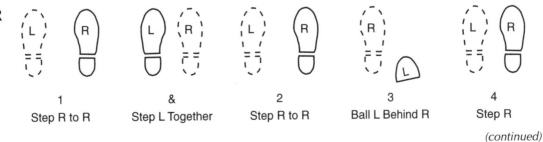

1	&	2	3	4
Step R to R	Step L Together	Step R to R	Ball L Behind R	Step R

(continued)

Elvira (continued)

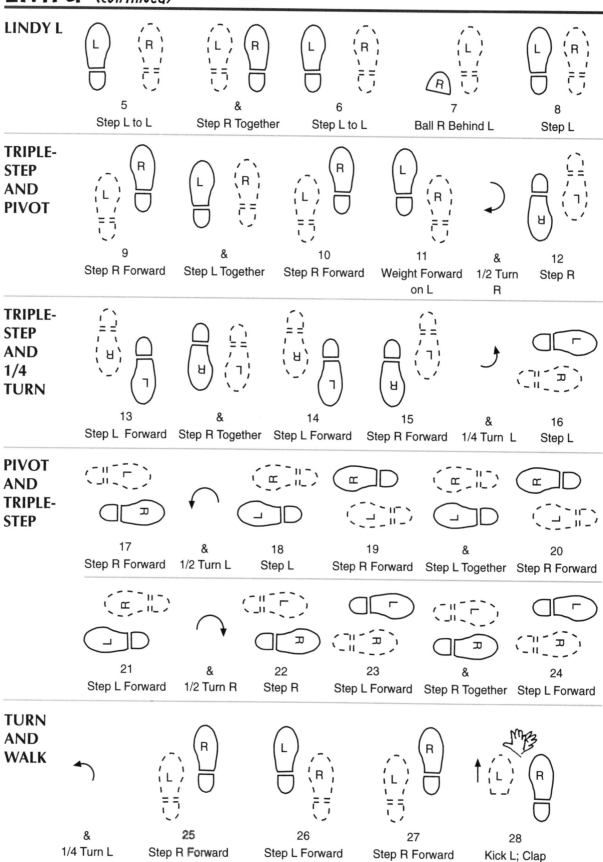

LINDY L

5	&	6	7	8
Step L to L	Step R Together	Step L to L	Ball R Behind L	Step L

TRIPLE-STEP AND PIVOT

9	&	10	11	&	12
Step R Forward	Step L Together	Step R Forward	Weight Forward on L	1/2 Turn R	Step R

TRIPLE-STEP AND 1/4 TURN

13	&	14	15	&	16
Step L Forward	Step R Together	Step L Forward	Step R Forward	1/4 Turn L	Step L

PIVOT AND TRIPLE-STEP

17	&	18	19	&	20
Step R Forward	1/2 Turn L	Step L	Step R Forward	Step L Together	Step R Forward

21	&	22	23	&	24
Step L Forward	1/2 Turn R	Step R	Step L Forward	Step R Together	Step L Forward

TURN AND WALK

&	25	26	27	28
1/4 Turn L	Step R Forward	Step L Forward	Step R Forward	Kick L; Clap

108

**WALK
BACK**

29

Step L Back

30

Step R Back

31

Step L Back

32

Stomp Together

Ball Change

R behind L.   Step L.

Honky Tonk Attitude

This dance is popular because it includes all of the most common line dance steps: touches, shuffles, jazz boxes, and stomps.

Music Suggestions

"Honky Tonk Attitude" by Joe Diffie

"Little Miss Honky Tonk" by Brooks and Dunn

"Honky Tonk Superman" by Aaron Tippin

Step Descriptions

1-4	Touch R heel forward, return to center, touch R toe to R side, return to center
5-8	Touch L heel forward, return to center, touch L toe to L side, return to center
9&10	Shuffle R (step R forward, step L together, step R forward)
11&12	Shuffle L (step L forward, step R together, step L forward)
13-16	Step R to R, step L to R, step R to R, tap L
17-20	Step L forward, pivot turn R and step R forward, stomp L foot twice next to R

21-24	Repeat counts 13-16
25-28	Repeat counts 17-20
29&30	Shuffle back R (step R back, step L together, step R back)
31&32	Shuffle back L (step L back, step R together, step L back)
33-36	Walk forward R, L, one-quarter turn L ending with feet together and hold one count
37-40	Jazz box L (cross R over L, step L back, step R to R, step L beside R)
41-44	Jazz box with one-quarter turn R (cross R over L, step L back, one-quarter turn R and step R, step L together)

Foot Map

HEEL, TOGETHER, TOE, TOGETHER

1	2	3	4
R Heel Forward	Together	R Toe to R Side	Together

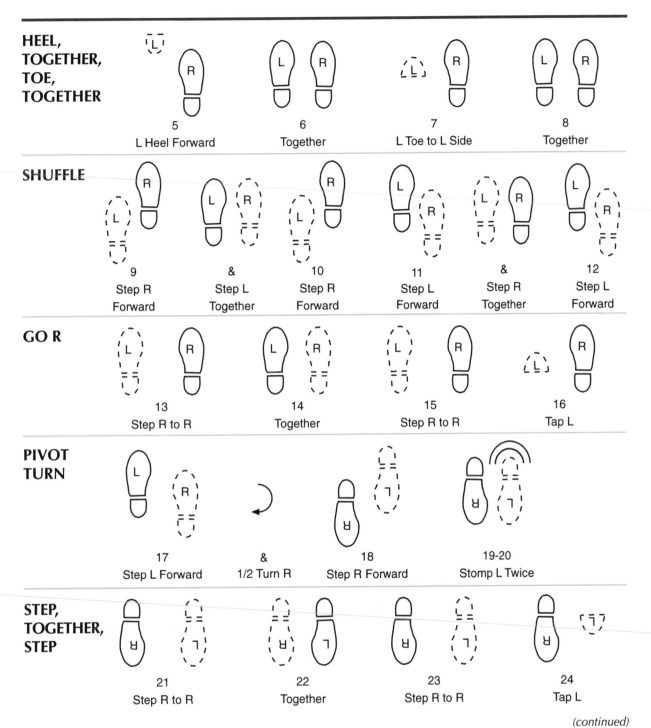

HEEL, TOGETHER, TOE, TOGETHER

5	6	7	8
L Heel Forward	Together	L Toe to L Side	Together

SHUFFLE

9	&	10	11	&	12
Step R Forward	Step L Together	Step R Forward	Step L Forward	Step R Together	Step L Forward

GO R

13	14	15	16
Step R to R	Together	Step R to R	Tap L

PIVOT TURN

17	&	18	19-20
Step L Forward	1/2 Turn R	Step R Forward	Stomp L Twice

STEP, TOGETHER, STEP

21	22	23	24
Step R to R	Together	Step R to R	Tap L

(continued)

Honky Tonk Attitude *(continued)*

PIVOT TURN AND STOMP

25	&	26	27-28
Step L Forward	1/2 Turn R	Step R Forward	Stomp L Together Twice

SHUFFLE BACK

29	&	30	31	&	32
Step R Back	Step L Together	Step R Back	Step L Back	Step R Together	Step L Back

WALK FORWARD AND TURN

33	34	&	35	36
Step R Forward	Step L Forward	1/4 Turn L	Step R	Hold

JAZZ BOX

37	38	39	40
Cross R Over L	Step L Back	Step R to R	Step L

41	42	&	43	44
Cross R Over L	Step L Back	1/4 Turn R	Step R to R	Step L in Place

Watermelon Crawl

This dance was choreographed to the famous song "Watermelon Crawl" by Tracy Byrd. The steps fit perfectly to the beat of the music. This dance became so popular that it showed up on my survey as one of the top 10 dances that everyone should know.

Music Suggestions

"Watermelon Crawl" by Tracy Byrd

"Shut Up and Kiss Me" by Mary Chapin Carpenter

"Why Haven't I Heard From You Lately?" by Reba McEntire

Step Descriptions

1-4   Turn R inward next to L with toes touching and heel off floor, touch R heel next to L, triple-step in place (R, L, R)

5-8   Turn L inward next to R with toes touching and heel off floor, touch L heel next to R, triple-step in place (L, R, L)

9-12   Charleston (step R forward, kick L and clap, step L back, touch R toe back and clap)

13-16   Repeat counts 9-12

17-20   Grapevine R (step R to R, cross L behind R, step R to R), kick L

21-24   Grapevine L (step L to L, cross R behind L, step L to L), one-quarter turn L, touch R and clap

25-28   One long step forward on R, slide L next to R for two counts and clap hands

29-32   One long step forward on L, slide R next to L for two counts and clap hands

33-36   Transfer weight to R as you lift L heel, lower L heel as you raise R heel, lower R heel as you raise L heel, lower L heel as you raise R heel

37-40   Full military turn (step R forward, pivot turn to L and step L forward, step R forward, pivot turn to L and step L forward)

Foot Map

TOE, HEEL

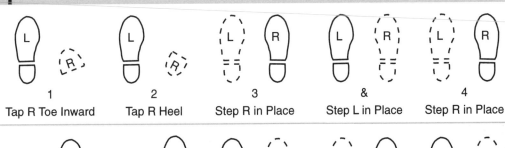

1	2	3	&	4
Tap R Toe Inward	Tap R Heel	Step R in Place	Step L in Place	Step R in Place

5	6	7	&	8
Tap L Toe Inward	Tap L Heel	Step L in Place	Step R in Place	Step L in Place

(continued)

Watermelon Crawl (continued)

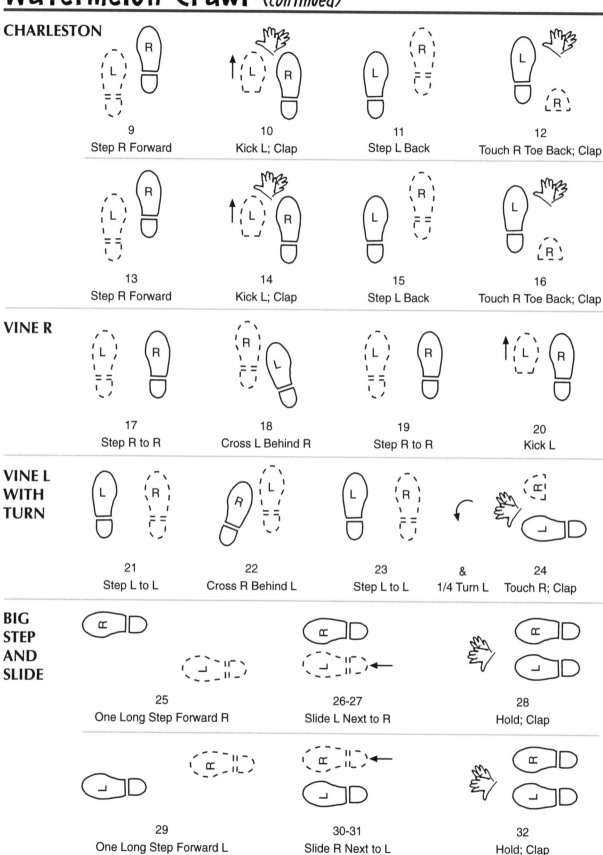

CHARLESTON

9	10	11	12
Step R Forward	Kick L; Clap	Step L Back	Touch R Toe Back; Clap

13	14	15	16
Step R Forward	Kick L; Clap	Step L Back	Touch R Toe Back; Clap

VINE R

17	18	19	20
Step R to R	Cross L Behind R	Step R to R	Kick L

VINE L WITH TURN

21	22	23	&	24
Step L to L	Cross R Behind L	Step L to L	1/4 Turn L	Touch R; Clap

BIG STEP AND SLIDE

25	26-27	28
One Long Step Forward R	Slide L Next to R	Hold; Clap

29	30-31	32
One Long Step Forward L	Slide R Next to L	Hold; Clap

HEELS UP

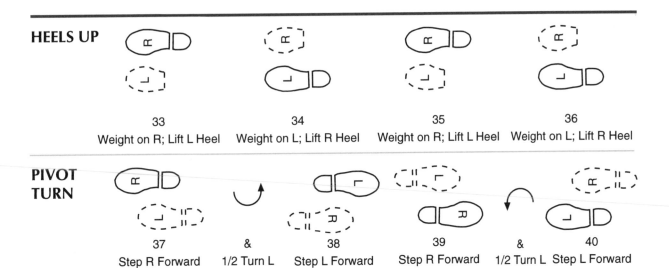

33	34	35	36
Weight on R; Lift L Heel	Weight on L; Lift R Heel	Weight on R; Lift L Heel	Weight on L; Lift R Heel

PIVOT TURN

37	&	38	39	&	40
Step R Forward	1/2 Turn L	Step L Forward	Step R Forward	1/2 Turn L	Step L Forward

Pivot Turn

Step L forward.   One-half turn R and step R forward.

Thunderfoot

This dance uses the drag step. A drag is similar to a slide, and a fabulous dancer named Fred Astaire used this movement quite often. Remember to keep your feet close to the ground as you perform this dance. Once you have it memorized, try to relax as you dance, especially during the drag step, and you will feel a "flow" that connects all the steps together. When performed fast, this dance is considered an advanced-level dance.

Music Suggestions

"Brand New Man" by Brooks and Dunn

"The Fireman" by George Strait

"Hillbilly Rock" by Marty Stuart

Step Descriptions

1-4   Touch R heel forward, hook R foot over L, touch R heel forward, step R next to L

5-8   Repeat 1-4 with L foot

9-12   One-quarter turn R and step R forward, drag L to R, step R forward, step L next to R

13-16   One-half turn L and step L forward, drag R to L, step L forward, touch R next to L

17-20   One-half turn R and step R forward, touch L next to R, one-half turn L and step L forward, step R next to L

21-24   Swivel R and one-half turn R, swivel L and one-half turn L, kick R twice

25-28   Walk back R, L, R, L

29-32   Step R forward, hook L over R, step L forward, hook R over L

33-36   Stomp R and put weight on R, stomp L ending with weight on both feet, swivel L, bring feet back to center

37-38   Swivel R and bring feet back to center

Variation

Perform this dance to 36 counts of music instead of 38 counts by eliminating the stomp R and stomp L in steps 33 and 34.

Foot Map

HEEL

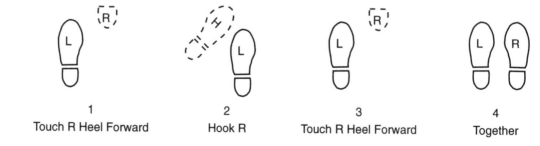

1	2	3	4
Touch R Heel Forward	Hook R	Touch R Heel Forward	Together

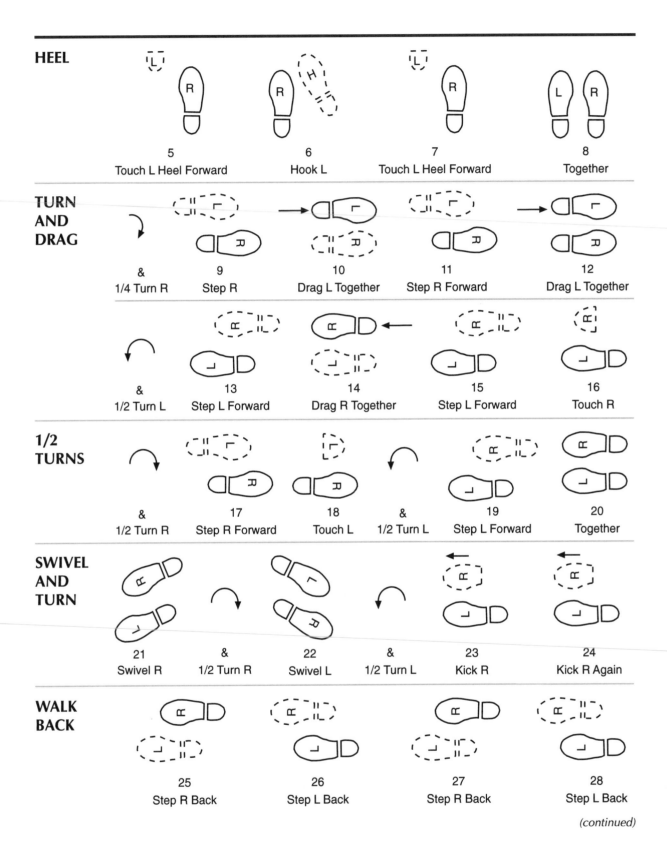

HEEL

5	6	7	8
Touch L Heel Forward	Hook L	Touch L Heel Forward	Together

TURN AND DRAG

&	9	10	11	12
1/4 Turn R	Step R	Drag L Together	Step R Forward	Drag L Together

&	13	14	15	16
1/2 Turn L	Step L Forward	Drag R Together	Step L Forward	Touch R

1/2 TURNS

&	17	18	&	19	20
1/2 Turn R	Step R Forward	Touch L	1/2 Turn L	Step L Forward	Together

SWIVEL AND TURN

21	&	22	&	23	24
Swivel R	1/2 Turn R	Swivel L	1/2 Turn L	Kick R	Kick R Again

WALK BACK

25	26	27	28
Step R Back	Step L Back	Step R Back	Step L Back

(continued)

117

Thunderfoot (continued)

FORWARD AND HOOK

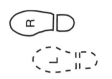  

29	30	31	32
Step R Forward	Hook L	Step L Forward	Hook R

STOMP AND SWIVEL

33	34	35	36
Stomp R	Stomp L	Swivel L	Together

SWIVEL

37	38
Swivel R	Together

Rock Around the Clock

The excitement of Big Band and '50s music has found its way to line dancing. Try this dance to different songs from these eras as well as to country-swing style songs.

Music Suggestions

"The Stroll" by the Diamonds

"In the Mood" by Glenn Miller

"Rock Around the Clock" by Bill Haley and the Comets

Step Descriptions

1-4	Touch R toe to R, touch R toe next to L, touch R toe to R, hold
5-8	Step R across L, step L to L, step R across L, hold
9-12	Touch L toe to L, touch L toe next to R, touch L toe to L, hold
13-16	Step L across R, step R to R, step L across R, hold
17-20	Rock forward R, step L back, step R beside L, hold
21-24	Step L back, slide R across L, step L, hold
25-28	Rock R back, step L forward, step R together, hold

29-32	Step L forward, slide R behind L with R arch next to L heel (small chug forward), step L forward, hold
33-36	Touch R beside L with R heel turned out, touch R heel beside L with R toe turned out, step R across L, hold
37-40	Touch L beside R with L heel turned out, touch L heel beside R with L toe turned out, step L across R, hold
41-44	Walk back R, L, step R forward, hold
45-48	Step L next to R and one-quarter turn L, step R forward and one-quarter turn L, step L forward and one-quarter turn L, hold

Foot Map

TOUCH R

1	2	3	4
Touch R Toe to R	Touch R Together	Touch R Toe to R	Hold

CROSS R

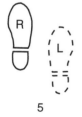   

5	6	7	8
Step R Across L	Step L to L	Step R Across L	Hold

(continued)

Rock Around the Clock (continued)

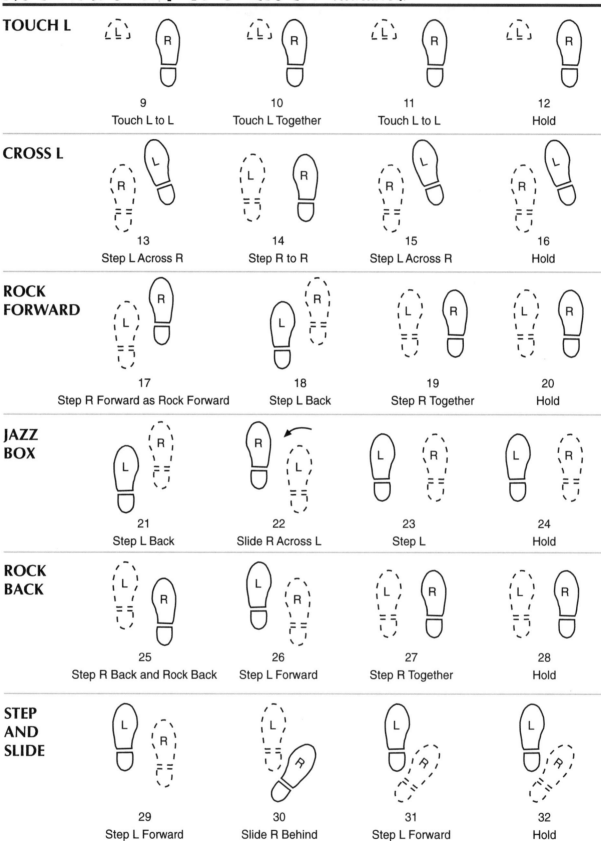

TOUCH L

9	10	11	12
Touch L to L	Touch L Together	Touch L to L	Hold

CROSS L

13	14	15	16
Step L Across R	Step R to R	Step L Across R	Hold

ROCK FORWARD

17	18	19	20
Step R Forward as Rock Forward	Step L Back	Step R Together	Hold

JAZZ BOX

21	22	23	24
Step L Back	Slide R Across L	Step L	Hold

ROCK BACK

25	26	27	28
Step R Back and Rock Back	Step L Forward	Step R Together	Hold

STEP AND SLIDE

29	30	31	32
Step L Forward	Slide R Behind	Step L Forward	Hold

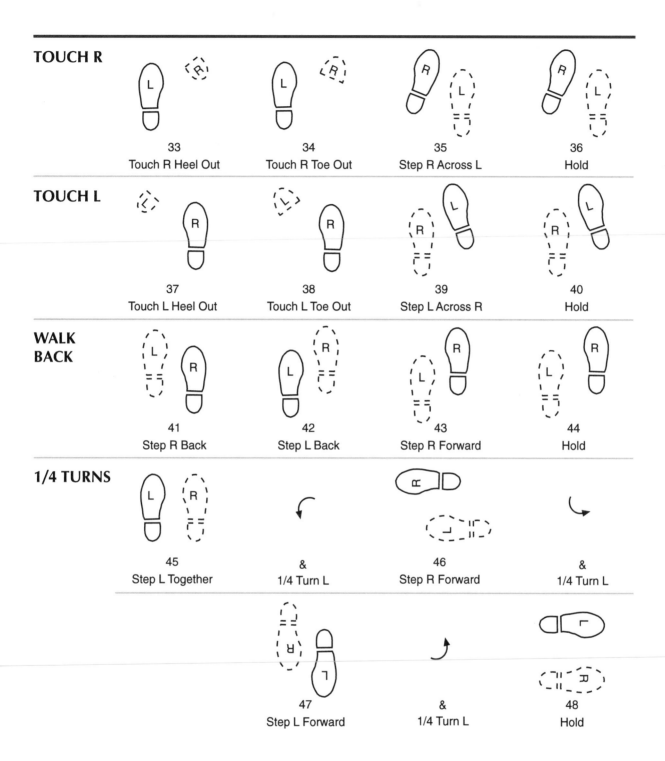

TOUCH R

33	34	35	36
Touch R Heel Out	Touch R Toe Out	Step R Across L	Hold

TOUCH L

37	38	39	40
Touch L Heel Out	Touch L Toe Out	Step L Across R	Hold

WALK BACK

41	42	43	44
Step R Back	Step L Back	Step R Forward	Hold

1/4 TURNS

45	&	46	&
Step L Together	1/4 Turn L	Step R Forward	1/4 Turn L

47	&	48
Step L Forward	1/4 Turn L	Hold

Dance Ranch Romp

**Four-Wall Dance
44 Counts**

Popular in Colorado and Florida, this dance begins with a step called a "grind" where the heel of your foot fans from side to side like you are grinding your heel into something.

Music Suggestions

"I Like It, I Love It" by Tim McGraw

"American Honky Tonk Bar Association" by Garth Brooks

"Restless" by Mark O'Connor

Step Descriptions

1-4   Step R heel forward pointing toes inward, "grind" or point toes outward keeping weight on R heel, step R back, step L next to R

5-8   Step L heel forward pointing toes inward, "grind" or point toes outward keeping weight on L heel, step L back, step R next to L

9-12   Step R forward, pivot turn L and step L, step R forward, pivot turn L and step L

13-16   Stomp R, stomp L, toe splits, toes together

17-20   Grapevine R (step R to R, step L behind R, step R to R), step L next to R

21-22   Toe splits, toes together

23-26   Grapevine L (step L to L, cross R behind L, step L to L), step R next to L

27-28   Toe splits, toes together

29-32   Step R forward, hitch L knee and scoot on R, step L back, step R together

33-36   Step L forward, lift R knee and scoot on L, step R back, step L together

37-40   Step R forward, one-quarter turn L and lift L knee and scoot forward, cross L over R, step R together

41-44   Stomp L in place, stomp R in place, slap palms of hands up and down for two counts

Variation

On counts 5 to 8, replace with a repeat of counts 1 to 4.

Foot Map

GRIND

 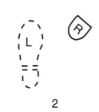  

1	2	3	4
R Heel Forward	Fan Out With R Heel	Step R Back	Step L Together

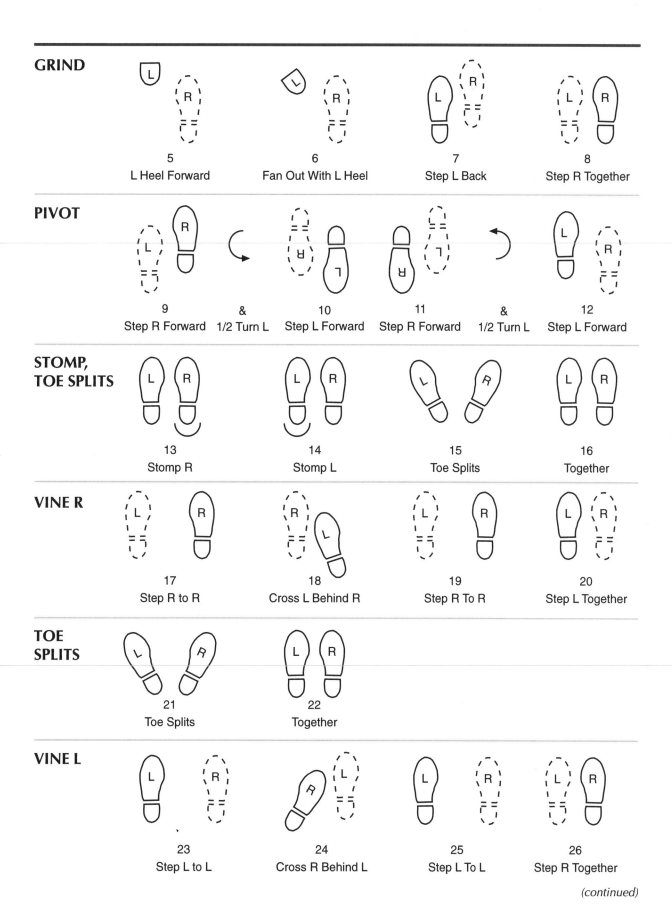

GRIND

5	6	7	8
L Heel Forward	Fan Out With L Heel	Step L Back	Step R Together

PIVOT

9	&	10	11	&	12
Step R Forward	1/2 Turn L	Step L Forward	Step R Forward	1/2 Turn L	Step L Forward

STOMP, TOE SPLITS

13	14	15	16
Stomp R	Stomp L	Toe Splits	Together

VINE R

17	18	19	20
Step R to R	Cross L Behind R	Step R To R	Step L Together

TOE SPLITS

21	22
Toe Splits	Together

VINE L

23	24	25	26
Step L to L	Cross R Behind L	Step L To L	Step R Together

(continued)

Dance Ranch Romp (continued)

TOE SPLITS

27
Toe Splits

28
Together

SCOOT R

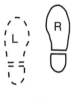

29
Step R Forward

30
Scoot R

31
Step L Back

32
Step R Together

SCOOT L

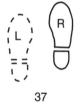

33
Step L Forward

34
Scoot L

35
Step R Back

36
Step L Together

FORWARD AND TURN

37
Step R Forward

&
1/4 Turn L

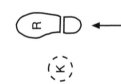

38
Scoot R

39
Cross L Over R

40
Step R Together

STOMP AND SLAP

41
Stomp L

42
Stomp R

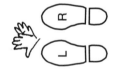

43-44
Slap Palms of Hands Up and Down

Alley Cat

Also known as Alley Walk, the origin of this dance can be traced back to the early 1980s. Throughout the years, the dance has been shortened slightly and modified. Here's the version popular today.

Music Suggestions

"Tulsa Time" by Don Williams

"I Feel Lucky" by Mary Chapin Carpenter

"Dumas Walker" by the Kentucky Headhunters

Step Descriptions

1-4	Swivel heels L, back to center, swivel heels L, back to center
5-8	Tap R heel forward, step together, tap R heel forward, step together
9-12	Swivel heels L, back to center, swivel heels L, back to center
13-16	Tap L heel forward, step together, tap L heel forward, step together
17-20	Step L forward, step R together, step L forward, step R together
21-24	Step L forward, step R together, step L forward, step R together
25-28	Step R diagonally back, stomp L next to R, step L diagonally back, stomp R together
29-32	Repeat counts 25-28
33-36	Take a big step R, hold one count, step L next to R, hold one count
37-40	Take a big step L, hold one count, step R next to L, hold one count
41-44	Kick ball change twice on R (kick R, step back on ball of R, step L in place and repeat)
45-48	Step R forward, step L together, tap L to side, stomp L next to R
49-52	Step L to L, cross R behind L, one-quarter turn L and step L, stomp R next to L
53-56	Walk back R, L, R, step L together

Variation

After count 40, repeat counts 37 to 40 before beginning count 41, thus adding four more counts to the dance.

Foot Map

SWIVEL

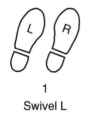
1
Swivel L

2
Center

3
Swivel L

4
Center

(continued)

Alley Cat (continued)

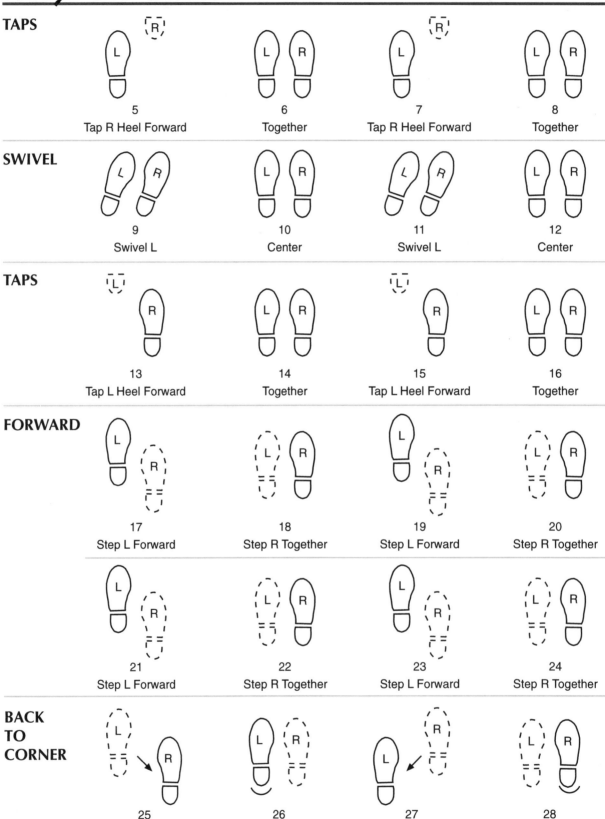

TAPS

5 — Tap R Heel Forward
6 — Together
7 — Tap R Heel Forward
8 — Together

SWIVEL

9 — Swivel L
10 — Center
11 — Swivel L
12 — Center

TAPS

13 — Tap L Heel Forward
14 — Together
15 — Tap L Heel Forward
16 — Together

FORWARD

17 — Step L Forward
18 — Step R Together
19 — Step L Forward
20 — Step R Together

21 — Step L Forward
22 — Step R Together
23 — Step L Forward
24 — Step R Together

BACK TO CORNER

25 — Step R Diagonal Back
26 — Stomp L Together
27 — Step L Diagonal Back
28 — Stomp R Together

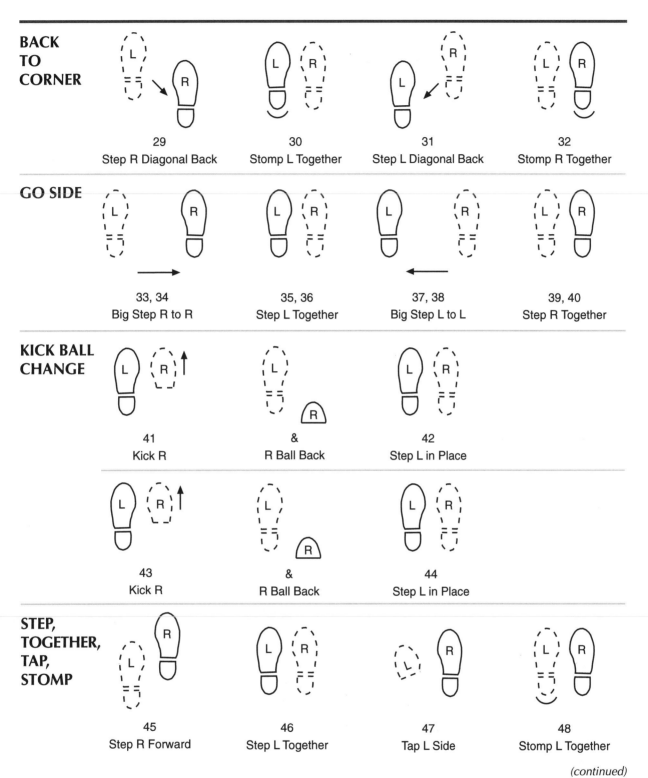

BACK TO CORNER

29	30	31	32
Step R Diagonal Back	Stomp L Together	Step L Diagonal Back	Stomp R Together

GO SIDE

33, 34	35, 36	37, 38	39, 40
Big Step R to R	Step L Together	Big Step L to L	Step R Together

KICK BALL CHANGE

41	&	42
Kick R	R Ball Back	Step L in Place

43	&	44
Kick R	R Ball Back	Step L in Place

STEP, TOGETHER, TAP, STOMP

45	46	47	48
Step R Forward	Step L Together	Tap L Side	Stomp L Together

(continued)

127

Alley Cat (continued)

VINE L WITH TURN

49	50	&	51	52
Step L to L	Cross R Behind L	1/4 Turn L	Step L	Stomp R Together

WALK BACK

53	54	55	56
Step R Back	Step L Back	Step R Back	Step L Together

Kick Ball Change

Kick L.   Step L.   Step R.

The Redneck

The Redneck originated in Virginia to the song "High Tech Redneck." You will enjoy dancing the first few steps some call the "Bug Squash." This dance also includes "shimmies"—that is, the ability to shake your shoulders while you dance.

Music Suggestions

"High Tech Redneck" by George Jones

"Dust on the Bottle" by David Lee Murphy

"Outta Here" by Shania Twain

Step Descriptions

1-4 Step forward on R heel with weight on heel and toes pointed L, point toes R and shift weight to L, step R together, step L in place

5-8 Repeat counts 1-4

9-11 Grapevine R (step R to R, cross L behind R, step R to R)

12-15 Step L forward, pivot turn R and step R forward, step L forward, pivot turn R and step R forward

16-18 Grapevine L (step L to L, step R behind L, step L to L)

19-22 Step R forward, pivot turn L and step L forward, step R forward, pivot turn L and step L forward

23&24 Shuffle R (step R forward, step L together, step R forward)

25&26 Shuffle L (step L forward, step R together, step L forward)

27-30 Chassé R (step R to R, step L together, step R to R), step L forward and rock back on R

31-34 Chassé L (step L to L, step R together, step L to L), chassé R (step R to R, step L together, step R to R)

35-38 Chassé L (step L to L, step R together, step L to L), step R back and rock forward L

39-42 Step R forward, one-quarter turn L and step L, stomp R together, hold and clap

43-46 Step R to R, shake hips and bend knees as you shimmy down and then back up for two counts, slide L foot next to R

47-50 Step L to L, shake hips and bend knees as you shimmy down and then back up for two counts, slide R foot next to L

51-54 Cross R over L, bend knees and spiral turn L, straighten up and lift heels off floor, lower heels to floor

55-56 With arms held straight out in front, pull arms back twice quickly as you push your hips forward.

Foot Map

BUG SQUASH

1	2	3	4
Step R Heel Forward; Point Toes L	Roll Heel so Toes Point R	Step R Together	Step L in Place

(continued)

The Redneck (continued)

BUG SQUASH

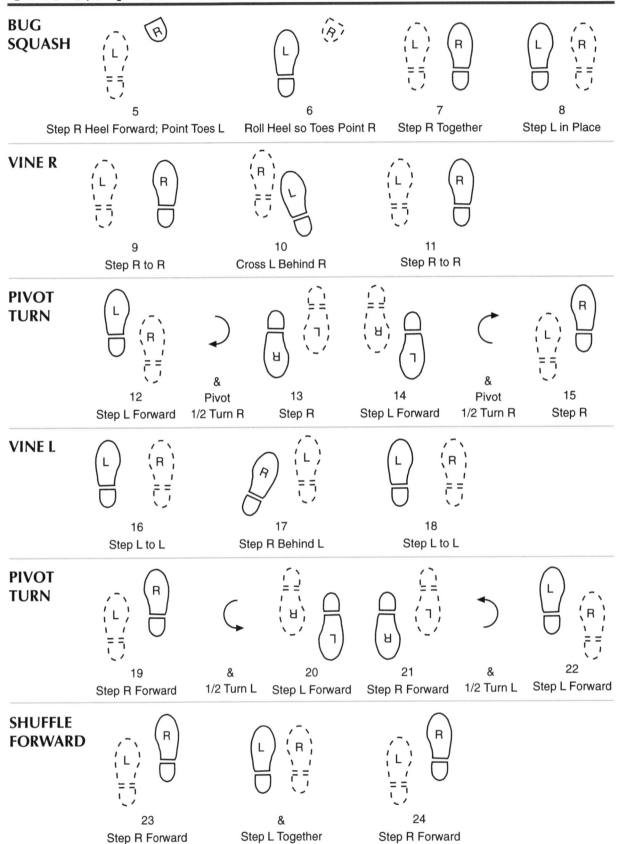

5	6	7	8
Step R Heel Forward; Point Toes L	Roll Heel so Toes Point R	Step R Together	Step L in Place

VINE R

9	10	11
Step R to R	Cross L Behind R	Step R to R

PIVOT TURN

12	&	13	14	&	15
Step L Forward	Pivot 1/2 Turn R	Step R	Step L Forward	Pivot 1/2 Turn R	Step R

VINE L

16	17	18
Step L to L	Step R Behind L	Step L to L

PIVOT TURN

19	&	20	21	&	22
Step R Forward	1/2 Turn L	Step L Forward	Step R Forward	1/2 Turn L	Step L Forward

SHUFFLE FORWARD

23	&	24
Step R Forward	Step L Together	Step R Forward

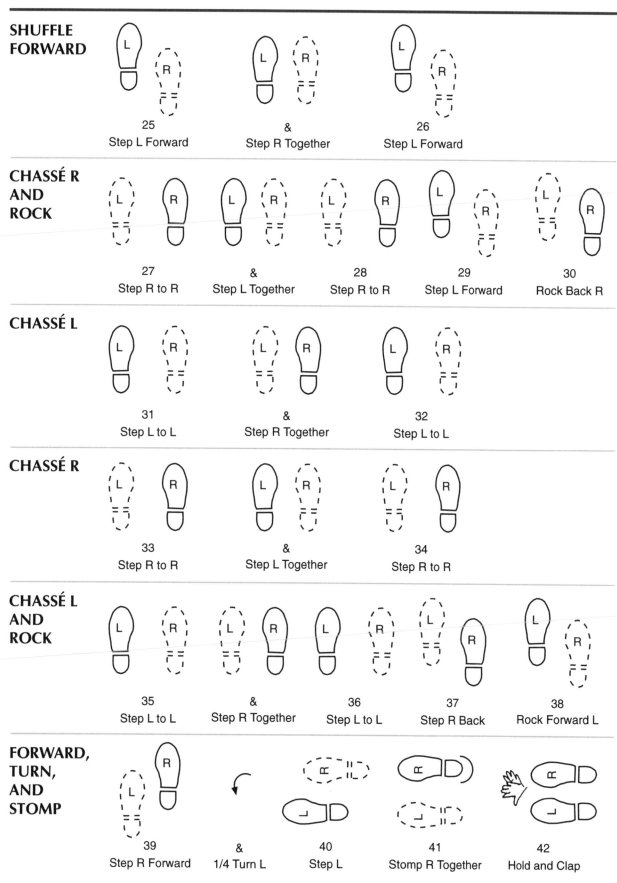

SHUFFLE FORWARD

25	&	26
Step L Forward	Step R Together	Step L Forward

CHASSÉ R AND ROCK

27	&	28	29	30
Step R to R	Step L Together	Step R to R	Step L Forward	Rock Back R

CHASSÉ L

31	&	32
Step L to L	Step R Together	Step L to L

CHASSÉ R

33	&	34
Step R to R	Step L Together	Step R to R

CHASSÉ L AND ROCK

35	&	36	37	38
Step L to L	Step R Together	Step L to L	Step R Back	Rock Forward L

FORWARD, TURN, AND STOMP

39	&	40	41	42
Step R Forward	1/4 Turn L	Step L	Stomp R Together	Hold and Clap

(continued)

The Redneck (continued)

SHAKE SHOULDERS

43	44	45	46
Step R to R	Shimmy Down	Shimmy Up	Slide L Together

47	48	49	50
Step L to L	Shimmy Down	Shimmy Up	Slide R Together

SPIRAL TURN

51	52	53	54
Cross R Over L	Bend Knees and Spiral Turn L	Straighten Legs and Lift Heels	Lower Heels to Floor

PULL ARMS BACK

55-56
Pull Arms Back Twice as
You Push Hips Forward Twice

Wild Wild West II

This dance grew in popularity with Will Smith's song, "Wild Wild West," released in the summer of 1999. Will Smith starred in the movie *Wild Wild West,* which was a modernized version of the old TV series.

Music Suggestion

"Wild Wild West" by Will Smith

Step Descriptions

1-4 One-quarter turn R and walk R, L, triple-step R (step R forward, step L together, step R forward)

5-8 One-half turn L and walk L, R, triple-step L (step L forward, step R together, step L forward)

9-12 One-quarter turn L and walk to the back R, L, triple step R (step R forward, step L together, step R forward)

13-16 Step L forward, pivot turn R, step R forward, triple-step L (step forward, step R together, step L forward)

17-20 Twist body R, L, then R, L, R in two counts (skate)

21-24 Twist body L, R, then L, R, L in two counts (skate)

25-28 Slide R (large step R, drag L to R), slide L (large step L, drag R to L)

29-32 Repeat counts 25-28, only add small "drumming" style movements

of the wrists. (This hand movement is sometimes called "Men in Black hands.")

33-36 One-quarter turn R and walk R, L, R, hold. On the last two counts punch fists out to side (R, L, R)

37-40 One-half turn L and walk L, R, L, hold. On the last two counts punch fists out to side (L, R, L)

41-44 One-quarter turn R, step R back, hold, step L back, hold

45-48 Walk forward R, L, kick ball change (kick R, hop on L, land on R, step L together)

49-52 Lean body to R side, L side, R side, L side with arms in a position as if driving a car. (For style, pretend you're tipping your hat as you are leaning side to side.)

53-56 Toe splits out and return to center, repeat three more times

Variations

1. On counts 13 to 16, replace with step L and pivot turn R, kick ball change (kick R, hop and land on R, hop and land on L).

2. On counts 39 to 40, substitute two funky pumps with L foot (pretend you are pumping a car brake with your heel).

3. On counts 41 to 44, rotate body when stepping back on R so the body is facing the R wall, then rotate the body to the L when stepping back on L so the body is facing the L wall.

Foot Map

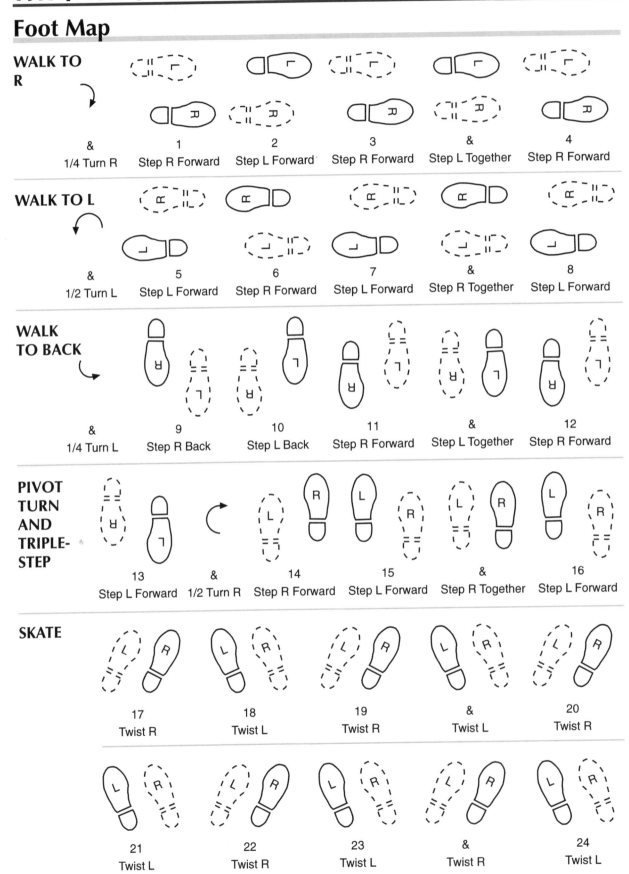

WALK TO R

&	1	2	3	&	4
1/4 Turn R	Step R Forward	Step L Forward	Step R Forward	Step L Together	Step R Forward

WALK TO L

&	5	6	7	&	8
1/2 Turn L	Step L Forward	Step R Forward	Step L Forward	Step R Together	Step L Forward

WALK TO BACK

&	9	10	11	&	12
1/4 Turn L	Step R Back	Step L Back	Step R Forward	Step L Together	Step R Forward

PIVOT TURN AND TRIPLE-STEP

13	&	14	15	&	16
Step L Forward	1/2 Turn R	Step R Forward	Step L Forward	Step R Together	Step L Forward

SKATE

17	18	19	&	20
Twist R	Twist L	Twist R	Twist L	Twist R

21	22	23	&	24
Twist L	Twist R	Twist L	Twist R	Twist L

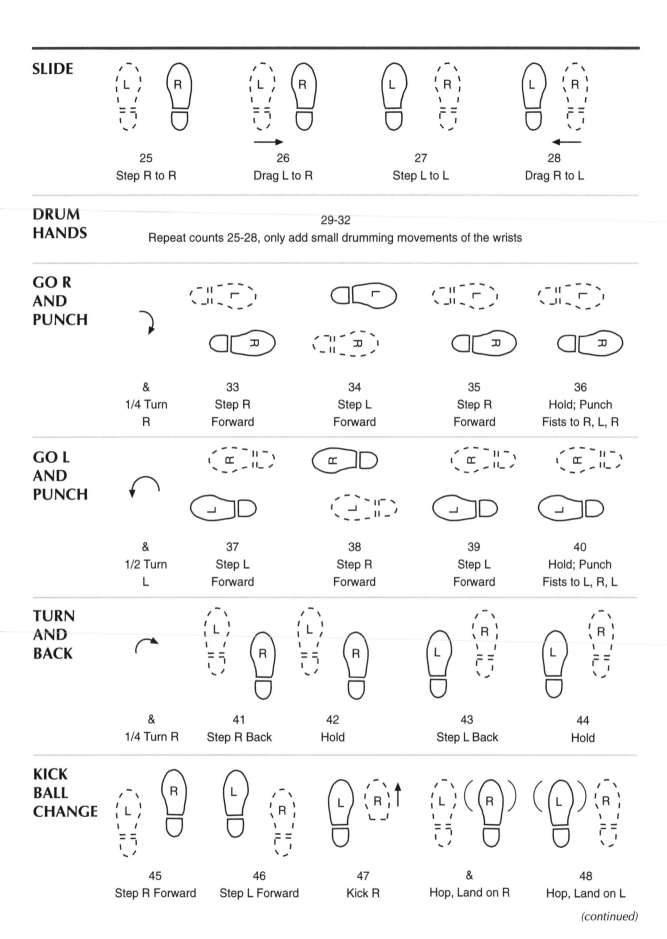

SLIDE

25	26	27	28
Step R to R	Drag L to R	Step L to L	Drag R to L

DRUM HANDS

29-32
Repeat counts 25-28, only add small drumming movements of the wrists

GO R AND PUNCH

&	33	34	35	36
1/4 Turn R	Step R Forward	Step L Forward	Step R Forward	Hold; Punch Fists to R, L, R

GO L AND PUNCH

&	37	38	39	40
1/2 Turn L	Step L Forward	Step R Forward	Step L Forward	Hold; Punch Fists to L, R, L

TURN AND BACK

&	41	42	43	44
1/4 Turn R	Step R Back	Hold	Step L Back	Hold

KICK BALL CHANGE

45	46	47	&	48
Step R Forward	Step L Forward	Kick R	Hop, Land on R	Hop, Land on L

(continued)

Wild Wild West II *(continued)*

LEAN TO SIDE

49	50	51	52
Lean Body to R Side	Lean to L	Lean to R	Lean to L

TOE SPLITS

53	&	54	&
Toe Splits	Center	Toe Splits	Center

55	&	56
Toe Splits	Center	Toe Splits

Toes out.   Center.

Livin' La Vida Loca

Ricky Martin became a superstar in 1999 with his release of the song "Livin' La Vida Loca," which means "living the crazy life." Don't let the number of counts scare you; quite a few of these steps are performed to two counts of music. This dance has a Latin style to it, so get ready to shake those hips!

Music Suggestion

"Livin' La Vida Loca" by Ricky Martin

Step Descriptions

1-4	Step R to R pushing hips to R, step L in place pushing hips to L, step R together, hold (Mambo side)
5-8	Step L to L pushing hips to L, step R in place pushing hips to R, step L together, hold (Mambo side)
9-16	Step R to R and clap hands or snap fingers up in air to L, step L in place and clap or snap up in air to R, step R in place and clap or snap low by L knee, step L in place and clap or snap low by R knee
17-20	Step R forward pushing hips to R, step L in place pushing hips to L, step R together, hold (Mambo forward)
21-24	Step L forward pushing hips to L, step R in place pushing hips R, step L together, hold (Mambo forward)
25-32	Repeat counts 9-16
33-40	Three-step turn R, stomp L
41-48	Three-step turn L, stomp R
49-52	Step R to R as rock hips R, rock hips L, rock hips R, hold
53-56	Step L in place as rock hips L, rock hips R, rock hips L, hold

57-60	Step R to R, hold, step L ball behind R, step R in place (salsa step)
61-64	Step L to L, hold, step R ball behind L, step L in place (salsa step)
65-68	Repeat steps 49-52
69-72	Repeat steps 53-56
73-76	Repeat steps 57-60
77-80	Repeat steps 61-64
81-84	Step R forward, hold, pivot turn L, step L forward
85-88	Repeat steps 81-84
89-92	Chassé R (step R to R, step L together, step R to R), hold
93-96	Chassé L (step L to L, step R together, step L to L), hold
97-100	Repeat steps 81-84
101-104	Repeat steps 85-88
105-108	Repeat steps 89-92
109-112	Repeat steps 93-96
113-120	Walk back R, hold, back L, hold, back R, hold, one-quarter turn L as step L and clap

Variations

1. On counts 33-40 and 41-48, replace the single three-step turns with double three-step turns.

2. On counts 49-64, replace with two jazz squares (cross R over L, hold, step L back, hold, step R back, hold, step L forward, hold, repeat).

Livin' La Vida Loca (continued)

Foot Map

MAMBO SIDE

Hips →	Hips ←		
1	2	3	4
Step R to R; Push Hips R	Step L in Place; Push Hips L	Step R Together	Hold

Hips ←	Hips →		
5	6	7	8
Step L to L; Push Hips L	Step R in Place; Push Hips R	Step L Together	Hold

CLAP

9, 10	11, 12	13, 14	15, 16
Step R to R; Clap or Snap Up to L	Step L in Place; Clap or Snap Up to R	Step R in Place; Clap or Snap Low to L	Step L in Place; Clap or Snap Low to R

MAMBO FORWARD

Hips →	Hips ←		
17	18	19	20
Step R Forward; Push Hips R	Step L in Place; Push Hips L	Step R Together	Hold

Hips ←	Hips →		
21	22	23	24
Step L Forward; Push Hips L	Step R in Place; Push Hips R	Step L Together	Hold

CLAP

25, 26	27, 28	29, 30	31, 32
Step R to R; Clap or Snap Up to L	Step L in Place; Clap or Snap Up to R	Step R in Place; Clap or Snap Low to L	Step L in Place; Clap or Snap Low to R

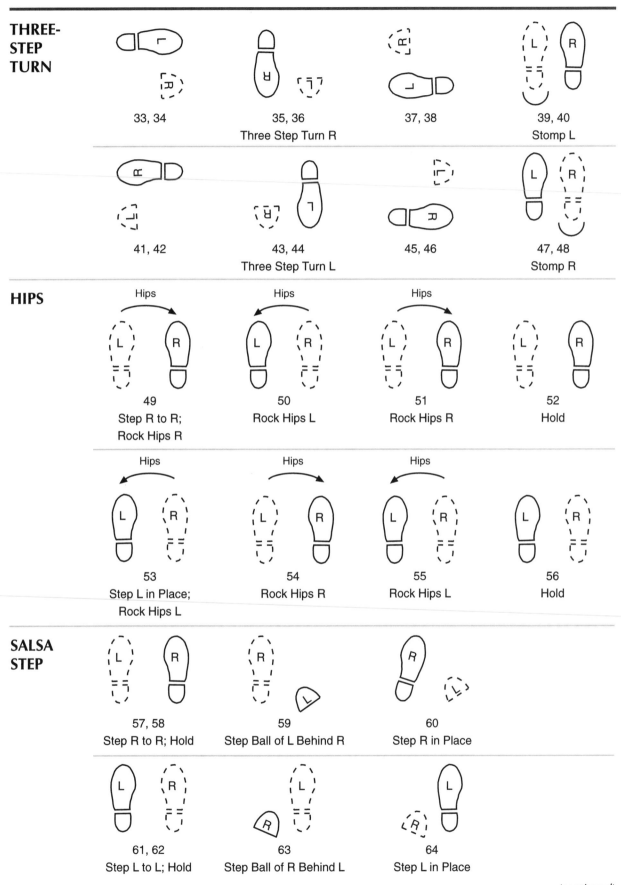

THREE-STEP TURN

33, 34 | 35, 36 Three Step Turn R | 37, 38 | 39, 40 Stomp L

41, 42 | 43, 44 Three Step Turn L | 45, 46 | 47, 48 Stomp R

HIPS

Hips | Hips | Hips

49 Step R to R; Rock Hips R | 50 Rock Hips L | 51 Rock Hips R | 52 Hold

Hips | Hips | Hips

53 Step L in Place; Rock Hips L | 54 Rock Hips R | 55 Rock Hips L | 56 Hold

SALSA STEP

57, 58 Step R to R; Hold | 59 Step Ball of L Behind R | 60 Step R in Place

61, 62 Step L to L; Hold | 63 Step Ball of R Behind L | 64 Step L in Place

(continued)

Livin' La Vida Loca *(continued)*

HIPS

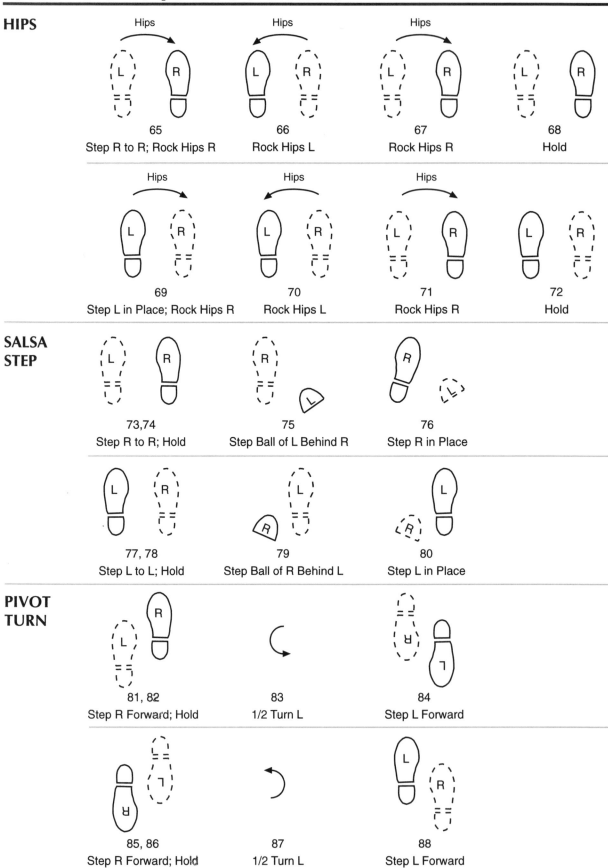

Hips

65	66	67	68
Step R to R; Rock Hips R	Rock Hips L	Rock Hips R	Hold

69	70	71	72
Step L in Place; Rock Hips R	Rock Hips L	Rock Hips R	Hold

SALSA STEP

73,74	75	76
Step R to R; Hold	Step Ball of L Behind R	Step R in Place

77, 78	79	80
Step L to L; Hold	Step Ball of R Behind L	Step L in Place

PIVOT TURN

81, 82	83	84
Step R Forward; Hold	1/2 Turn L	Step L Forward

85, 86	87	88
Step R Forward; Hold	1/2 Turn L	Step L Forward

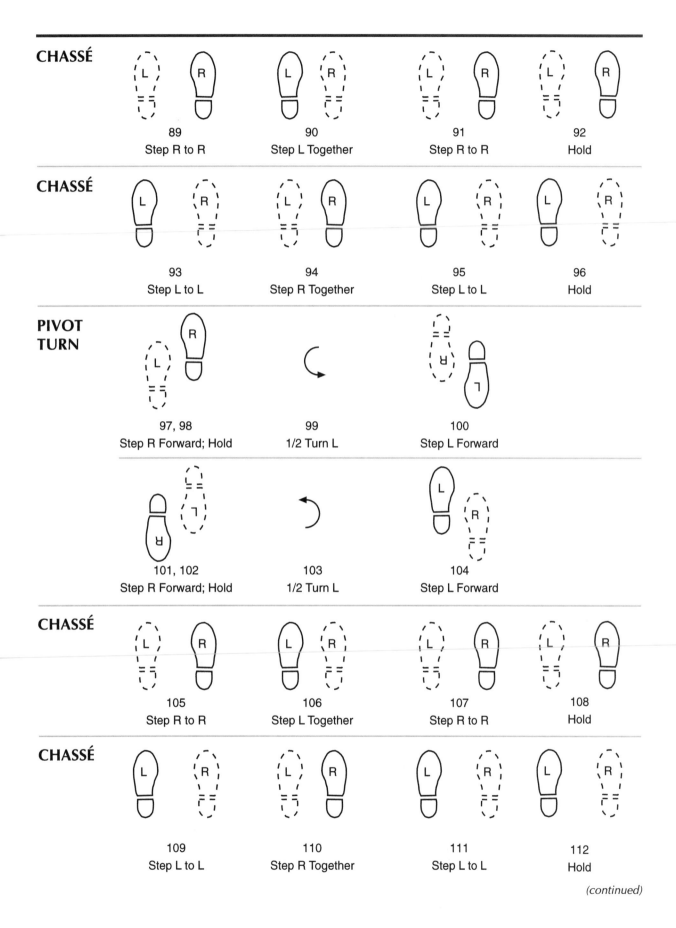

CHASSÉ

89	90	91	92
Step R to R	Step L Together	Step R to R	Hold

CHASSÉ

93	94	95	96
Step L to L	Step R Together	Step L to L	Hold

PIVOT TURN

97, 98	99	100
Step R Forward; Hold	1/2 Turn L	Step L Forward

101, 102	103	104
Step R Forward; Hold	1/2 Turn L	Step L Forward

CHASSÉ

105	106	107	108
Step R to R	Step L Together	Step R to R	Hold

CHASSÉ

109	110	111	112
Step L to L	Step R Together	Step L to L	Hold

(continued)

Livin' La Vida Loca *(continued)*

WALK BACK

113, 114	115, 116	117, 118
Step R Back; Hold	Step L Back; Hold	Step R Back; Hold

TURN AND CLAP

119
1/4 Turn L

120
Step L; Clap

Pivot Turn

Step L forward.

One-half turn R and step R forward.

The Gilley

Are you ready for some different types of turns? On the last four counts of this dance you will be performing one-third turns three times to complete a full 360-degree turn. Good luck!

Music Suggestions

"Stagger Lee" by Mickey Gilley

"Play Ruby Play" by Mickey Gilley

"She Used to Be Somebody's Baby" by the Gatlin Brothers

Step Descriptions

1-4   Touch R toe forward (toe outward), touch R heel forward (toe inward), cross R over L, slide L forward and end with instep behind R heel

5-8   Step R forward, cross L behind R, step R to R, cross L over R and one-quarter turn R

9-11   Step R forward, touch L heel forward, one-quarter turn R and step L to L

12-16   Cross R behind L, step L to L, stomp R, kick R, step R in place, step L in place

17-20   Step R forward, cross L behind R, pivot turn R and step R forward, step L together

21-24   Step R forward and push hips R, push hips R again, shift weight to L and push hips L, push hips L again

25-28   Step R back, rock weight forward onto L, step R forward, cross L behind R

29-32   Step R forward and one-quarter turn R, make a 360-degree turn by crossing L over R and one-third turn R, cross R behind L and one-third turn R, cross L over R and one-third turn R

Foot Map

TOE, HEEL, CROSS, AND SLIDE

1
Touch R Toe

2
Touch R Heel

3
Cross R Over L

4
Slide L Behind R

CROSS

5
Step R Forward

6
Cross L Behind R

7
Step R to R

8
Cross L Over R

&
1/4 Turn R

(continued)

The Gilley (continued)

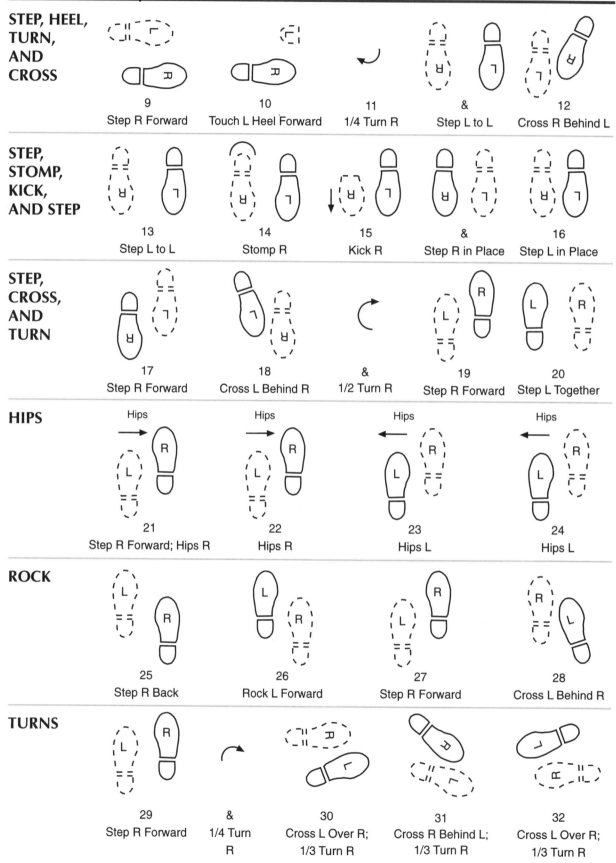

STEP, HEEL, TURN, AND CROSS

9	10	11	&	12
Step R Forward	Touch L Heel Forward	1/4 Turn R	Step L to L	Cross R Behind L

STEP, STOMP, KICK, AND STEP

13	14	15	&	16
Step L to L	Stomp R	Kick R	Step R in Place	Step L in Place

STEP, CROSS, AND TURN

17	18	&	19	20
Step R Forward	Cross L Behind R	1/2 Turn R	Step R Forward	Step L Together

HIPS

21	22	23	24
Step R Forward; Hips R	Hips R	Hips L	Hips L

ROCK

25	26	27	28
Step R Back	Rock L Forward	Step R Forward	Cross L Behind R

TURNS

29	&	30	31	32
Step R Forward	1/4 Turn R	Cross L Over R; 1/3 Turn R	Cross R Behind L; 1/3 Turn R	Cross L Over R; 1/3 Turn R

144

Waltz Across Texas

The waltz is a very old form of dance that came from Europe many centuries ago. It was originally a partner dance where long gowns and fancy clothes were worn. Now country dancers are doing a freestyle waltz. All waltz line dances are performed to "1-2-3" waltz music. Stay light on your feet when performing this dance and go where the music takes you. Even though this is a line dance, it can also be a partner dance.

Music Suggestions

"I See It Now" by Tracy Lawrence

"Waltz Across Texas" by Willie Nelson/ Ernest Tubbs

"Dream on Texas Ladies" by John Michael Montgomery

Step Descriptions

1-3	Cross L over R, step R back, step L next to R
4-6	Cross R over L, step L back, step R next to L
7-9	Step L forward, step R next to L, step L in place
10-12	Step R forward, step L next to R, step R in place
13-15	Step L back, step R back, step L next to R
16-18	Step R back, step L back, step R next to L
19-21	Step L to L, cross R behind L, step L to L
22-24	Cross R over L, step L to L, cross R behind L

25-27	Step L to L and sway L, sway R, sway L
28-30	Step R to R, cross L behind R, step R to R
31-33	Cross L over R, step R to R, cross L behind R
34-36	Step R to R and sway R, sway L, sway R
37-39	Step L forward and one-half turn L picking up R leg, step R next to L, step L in place
40-42	Step R back, step L next to R, step R in place
43-45	Step L forward and one-half turn L picking up R leg, step R next to L, step L in place
46-48	Step R back, step L next to R, step R in place

Variation

Replace counts 19 to 21 with a rolling grapevine L; replace counts 28 to 30 with a rolling grapevine R.

Foot Map

CROSS L

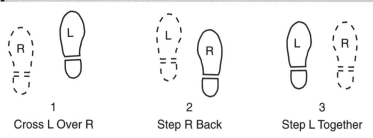

1	2	3
Cross L Over R	Step R Back	Step L Together

(continued)

Waltz Across Texas (continued)

CROSS R

4

Cross R Over L

5

Step L Back

6

Step R Together

STEP, TOGETHER

7

Step L Forward

8

Step R Together

9

Step L In Place

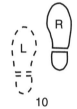

10

Step R Forward

11

Step L Together

12

Step R In Place

BACK L

13

Step L Back

14

Step R Back

15

Step L Together

BACK R

16

Step R Back

17

Step L Back

18

Step R Together

GO LEFT

19

Step L to L

20

Cross R Behind L

21

Step L to L

146

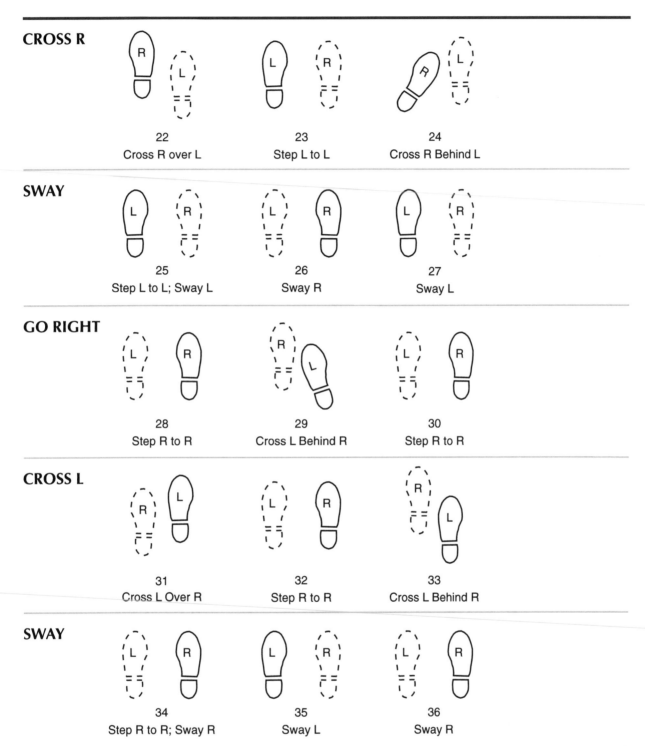

CROSS R

22
Cross R over L

23
Step L to L

24
Cross R Behind L

SWAY

25
Step L to L; Sway L

26
Sway R

27
Sway L

GO RIGHT

28
Step R to R

29
Cross L Behind R

30
Step R to R

CROSS L

31
Cross L Over R

32
Step R to R

33
Cross L Behind R

SWAY

34
Step R to R; Sway R

35
Sway L

36
Sway R

(continued)

Waltz Across Texas (continued)

STEP AND TURN

37	&	38	39
Step L Forward, Lifting R Leg	1/2 Turn L	Step R Together	Step L in Place

BACK, TOGETHER

40	41	42
Step R Back	Step L Together	Step R in Place

STEP, TURN

43	&	44	45
Step L Forward	1/2 Turn L	Step R Together	Step L in Place

BACK

46	47	48
Step R Back	Step L Together	Step R in Place

A favorite for line dancers that like funky-style movements, this dance consists of upper-body movements as well as a lot of footwork to give it the hip-hop style.

Music Suggestions

"Funky Cowboy" by Ronnie McDowell

"Rock Bottom" by Wynonna Judd

Any current funky tune on the music charts today

Step Descriptions

1-4	Lift R knee and cross knee over L leg, touch R toe to R, lift R knee and cross over L leg again, touch R toe to R again
5-8	Touch R heel over L, touch R heel toward 2 o'clock, touch R heel over L, step R together
9-12	Stomp L, one-quarter turn R and touch R heel forward, step R together, touch L heel forward
13-16	Cross L behind R, cross R behind L, cross L behind R, rock R forward, rock L back (Roger Rabbit)
17-20	Step R forward and roll hips R, one-quarter turn L and roll hips L, roll hips R again, roll hips L again
21-24	Step R together, touch L heel forward, step L together, touch R toe forward and hold
25-28	Tap R toe to side, circle knee to R and bring R heel down, tap L toe to side, circle knee to L and bring L heel down

29-32	Roll R knee to R, roll L knee to L, bend knees together, bend knees apart and then together again
33-36	Step R to R, drag L together, step R to R, drag L together
37-40	One-quarter turn R and step L forward, touch R next to L, step R forward, touch L next to R
&41& 42	Jump on L to L, jump feet apart onto R, step L together, step R across L
43-44	Spiral turn 180 degrees L (end with feet apart), hold
&45& 46	Reach arms forward, pull fists in, reach arms forward, pull fists in
47-48	Roll body from bottom to top for two counts by pushing the knees forward, then the hips, then the chest, then the head

Foot Map

LIFT KNEE AND TAP

1	2	3	4
Lift R Knee Across L	Touch R to Side	Lift R Knee Across L	Touch R to Side

(continued)

Funky Cowboy II (continued)

HEELS

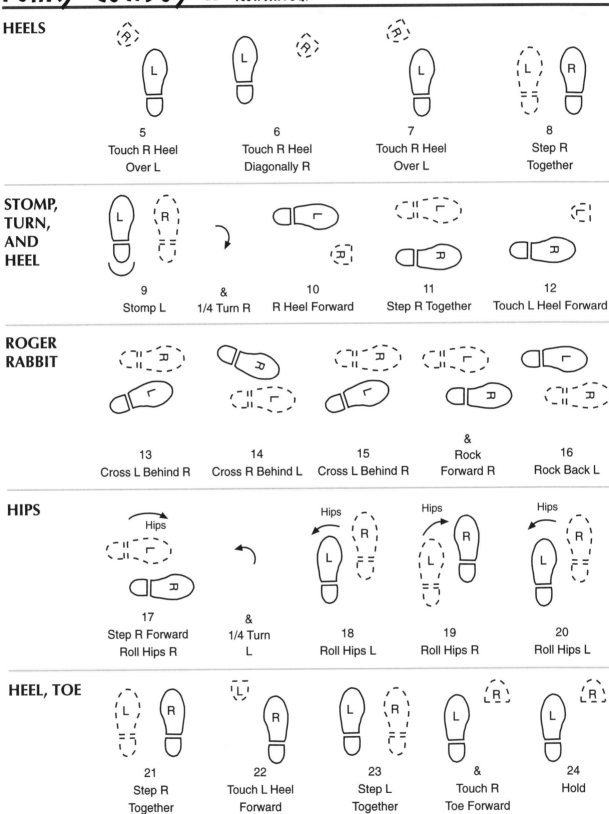

5	6	7	8
Touch R Heel Over L	Touch R Heel Diagonally R	Touch R Heel Over L	Step R Together

STOMP, TURN, AND HEEL

9	&	10	11	12
Stomp L	1/4 Turn R	R Heel Forward	Step R Together	Touch L Heel Forward

ROGER RABBIT

13	14	15	&	16
Cross L Behind R	Cross R Behind L	Cross L Behind R	Rock Forward R	Rock Back L

HIPS

17	&	18	19	20
Step R Forward Roll Hips R	1/4 Turn L	Roll Hips L	Roll Hips R	Roll Hips L

HEEL, TOE

21	22	23	&	24
Step R Together	Touch L Heel Forward	Step L Together	Touch R Toe Forward	Hold

150

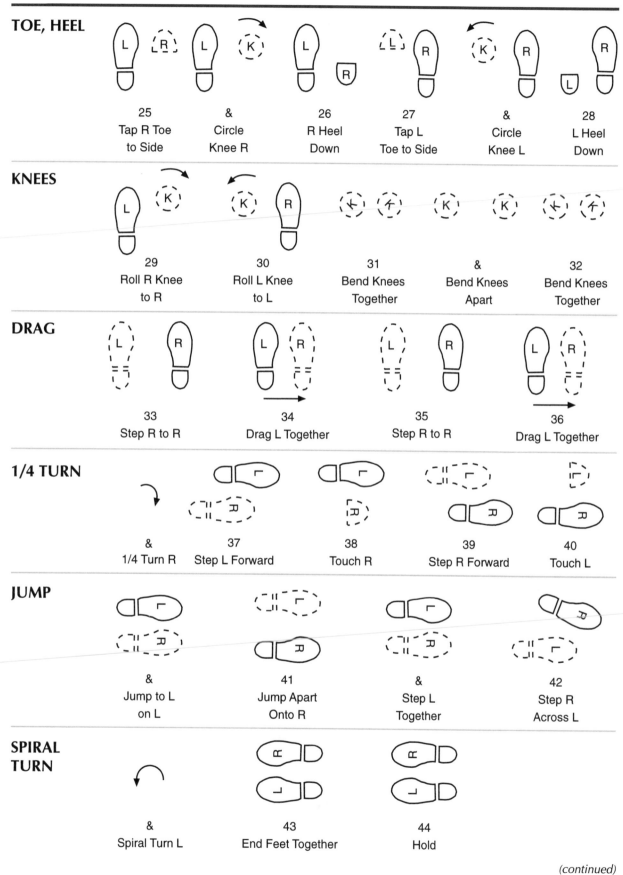

TOE, HEEL

25	&	26	27	&	28
Tap R Toe to Side	Circle Knee R	R Heel Down	Tap L Toe to Side	Circle Knee L	L Heel Down

KNEES

29	30	31	&	32
Roll R Knee to R	Roll L Knee to L	Bend Knees Together	Bend Knees Apart	Bend Knees Together

DRAG

33	34	35	36
Step R to R	Drag L Together	Step R to R	Drag L Together

1/4 TURN

&	37	38	39	40
1/4 Turn R	Step L Forward	Touch R	Step R Forward	Touch L

JUMP

&	41	&	42
Jump to L on L	Jump Apart Onto R	Step L Together	Step R Across L

SPIRAL TURN

&	43	44
Spiral Turn L	End Feet Together	Hold

(continued)

Funky Cowboy II (continued)

PULL FISTS

      &   **45**   **&**   **46**

Reach Arms Forward   Pull Fists In   Reach Arms Forward   Pull Fists In

BODY ROLL

     47   **48**

Body Roll   Continue Body Roll

 **Heel**

When You Really Get Good...

Advanced Line Dances

Are you ready to try a 96-count line dance? Sure you are! Just pretend it's three line dances put together. What makes a line dance advanced is the length of the dance, the specialty footwork (like a syncopated toe and heel step), the speed of the dance, or the definite style that is the trademark of the original dance. If you can master these dances at a fast speed, you are *good!* By now, you have probably noticed that consistent repetition will help your subconscious memorize the steps so that you can just flow through the moves. So if you have mastered the earlier dances and are ready for more of a challenge, these dances are for you!

Achy Breaky	166	Hip-Hop	174
Boot Scoot Boogie II	155	LeDoux Shuffle	169
CHES	180	Romeo	163
Cowboy Cha-Cha	161	Walkin' Wazi	158

Boot Scoot Boogie II

People everywhere went wild when they heard the upbeat and fun song "Boot Scootin' Boogie" by Brooks and Dunn. In fact, many people choreographed their own versions of line dances to match this song that made it to the top of the charts. If there were a contest for a dance with the most variations, this would be voted number one. Here is a very popular version that originated in Idaho.

Music Suggestions

"Boot Scootin' Boogie" by Brooks and Dunn

"Lost and Found" by Brooks and Dunn

"When She Cries" by Restless Heart

Step Descriptions

1-4	Tap R heel forward, hook R, tap R heel forward, step R together
5-8	Toe fan L, return to center, hook L and scoot R twice
9-12	Grapevine L (step L to L, cross R behind L, step L to L), kick R
13-16	Grapevine R (step R to R, cross L behind R, step R to R), stomp L
17-20	Turn in L toe and tap beside R, one-quarter turn L and tap L heel forward, hook L and scoot R twice

21-24	Grapevine L (step L to L, cross R behind L, step L to L), scuff R making a small circle with foot to R
25-28	Step R to R, scuff L making a small circle with foot to L, step L to L, scuff R making a small circle with foot to R
29-32	Cross R over L, step L to L, tap R behind L, stomp R

Variation

Substitute single or double rolling grapevines for any of the grapevines.

Foot Map

HEEL

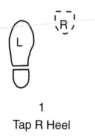
1
Tap R Heel

2
Hook R

3
Tap R Heel

4
Together

(continued)

Boot Scoot Boogie II (continued)

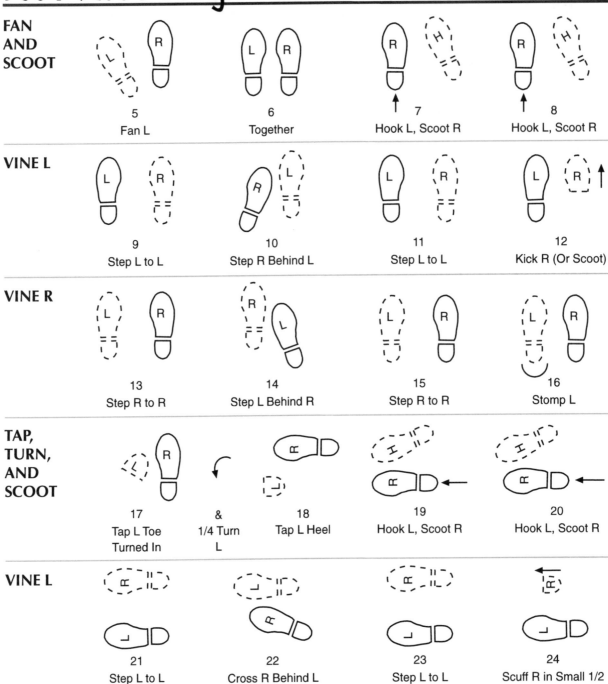

FAN AND SCOOT

5	6	7	8
Fan L	Together	Hook L, Scoot R	Hook L, Scoot R

VINE L

9	10	11	12
Step L to L	Step R Behind L	Step L to L	Kick R (Or Scoot)

VINE R

13	14	15	16
Step R to R	Step L Behind R	Step R to R	Stomp L

TAP, TURN, AND SCOOT

17	&	18	19	20
Tap L Toe Turned In	1/4 Turn L	Tap L Heel	Hook L, Scoot R	Hook L, Scoot R

VINE L

21	22	23	24
Step L to L	Cross R Behind L	Step L to L	Scuff R in Small 1/2 Circle to R

STEP, SCUFF

25	26	27	28
Step R to R	Scuff L in Small 1/2 Circle to L	Step L to L	Scuff R in Small 1/2 Circle to R

CROSS, SIDE, TAP, AND STOMP

29	30	31	32
Cross R Over L	Step L to L	Tap R Behind L	Stomp R

Toe out.

Together.

Walkin' Wazi

One of the line dance greats.

Music Suggestions

"Dumas Walker" by the Kentucky Headhunters

"Vickie Vance Gotta Dance" by Mark Chesnutt

"Honky Tonk Blues" by the Pirates of the Mississippi

Step Descriptions

1-4	Lift R heel and drop it twice, lift L heel and drop it twice
5-8	Kick R forward twice, step R back, tap L back
9-10	Step L forward, one-quarter turn L and step R together
11-14	Repeat counts 1-4
15-18	Repeat counts 5-8
19-20	Repeat counts 9-10
21-24	Traveling grapevine R (step R to R, cross L behind R, step R to R, cross L over R)

25-28	Traveling grapevine R (step R to R, cross L behind R, step R to R, cross L over R)
29-32	One-quarter turn L and hitch R, step R forward, shift weight back on L, shift weight forward on R
33-36	Step L forward, pivot turn R and step R forward, step L forward, pivot turn R and step R forward
37-40	Step L forward, pivot turn R and step R forward, step L forward, stomp R together ending with weight on both feet

Variation

On count 38, replace the pivot turn with a quarter turn, thus making it a two-wall dance.

Foot Map

HEEL 2
KICK 2

1, 2
Lift R Heel and
Drop It Twice

3, 4
Lift L Heel and
Drop It Twice

5
Kick R Forward

6
Kick R Forward

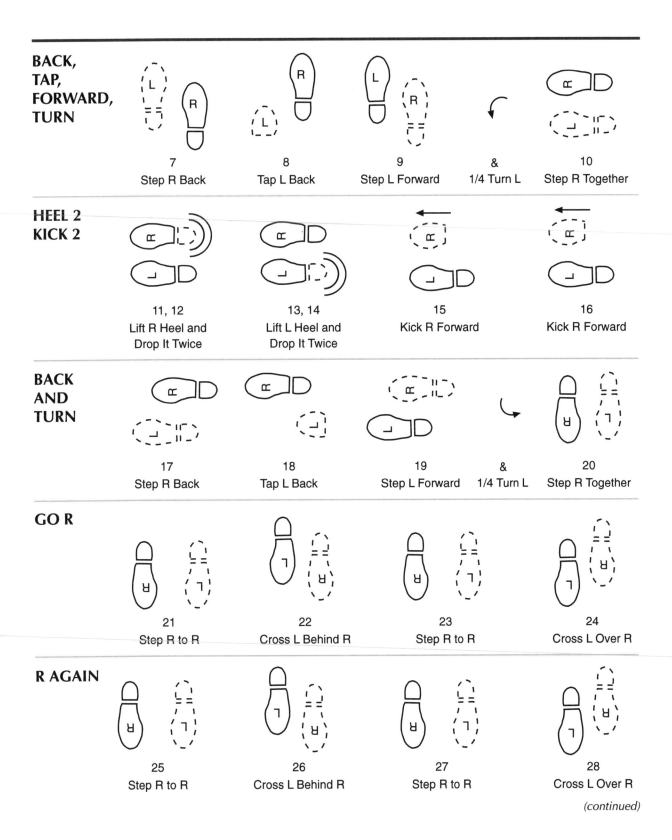

BACK, TAP, FORWARD, TURN

7	8	9	&	10
Step R Back	Tap L Back	Step L Forward	1/4 Turn L	Step R Together

HEEL 2 KICK 2

11, 12	13, 14	15	16
Lift R Heel and Drop It Twice	Lift L Heel and Drop It Twice	Kick R Forward	Kick R Forward

BACK AND TURN

17	18	19	&	20
Step R Back	Tap L Back	Step L Forward	1/4 Turn L	Step R Together

GO R

21	22	23	24
Step R to R	Cross L Behind R	Step R to R	Cross L Over R

R AGAIN

25	26	27	28
Step R to R	Cross L Behind R	Step R to R	Cross L Over R

(continued)

159

Walkin' Wazi (continued)

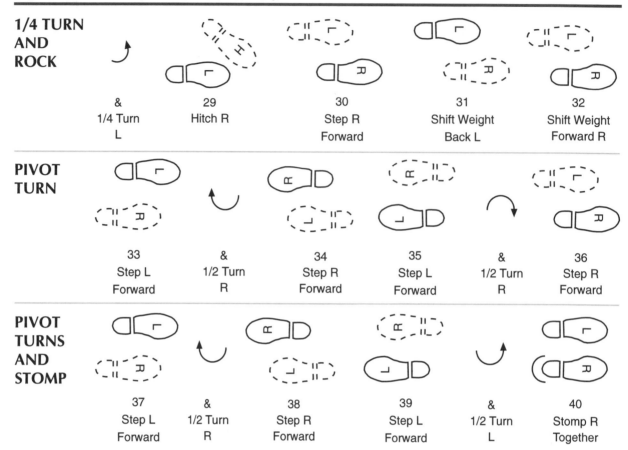

1/4 TURN AND ROCK

&	29	30	31	32
1/4 Turn L	Hitch R	Step R Forward	Shift Weight Back L	Shift Weight Forward R

PIVOT TURN

33	&	34	35	&	36
Step L Forward	1/2 Turn R	Step R Forward	Step L Forward	1/2 Turn R	Step R Forward

PIVOT TURNS AND STOMP

37	&	38	39	&	40
Step L Forward	1/2 Turn R	Step R Forward	Step L Forward	1/2 Turn L	Stomp R Together

Stomp

Together.   Lift foot.   Stomp together.

160

Cowboy Cha-Cha

Cha-cha dances are performed to cha-cha style music. This dance has been called the Stationary Cha-Cha. There are many variations throughout the U.S. It can also be a partner-pattern dance with couples beginning in dancing skaters' position (see page 183).

Music Suggestions

"Neon Moon" by Brooks and Dunn

"Old Country" by Mark Chesnutt

"My Maria" by Brooks and Dunn

Step Descriptions

1-2 Step R forward and rock forward, shift weight back onto L

3&4 Shuffle back R (step R back, step L together, step R back)

5-6 Step L back and rock back, shift weight to R

7&8 One-quarter turn R and step L to L, step R together, one-quarter turn R and step L back

9-10 Step R back and rock back, return weight to L

11&12 One-quarter turn L and step R to R, step L together, one-quarter turn L and step R back

13-14 Step L back and rock back, shift weight to R

15&16 One-quarter turn R, shuffle forward L (step L forward, step R together, step L forward)

17-18 Step R forward, pivot turn L and step L forward

19&20 Shuffle forward R (step R forward, step L together, step R forward)

21-22 Step L forward, pivot turn R and step R forward

23-24 Step L forward, step R back and rock back

25-26 Step L forward and rock forward, step R back and rock back

27&28 Shuffle forward L (step L forward, step R together, step L forward)

Foot Map

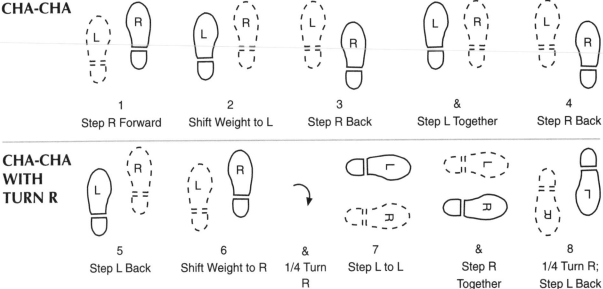

(continued)

Cowboy Cha-Cha (continued)

CHA-CHA WITH TURN L

 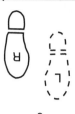    

9	10	&	11	&	12
Step R Back; Rock Back	Shift Weight to L	1/4 Turn L	Step R to R	Step L Together	1/4 Turn L; Step R Back

CHA-CHA WITH TURN R

13	14	&	15	&	16
Step L Back; Rock Back	Shift Weight to R	1/4 Turn R	Step L Forward	Step R Together	Step L Forward

STEP, 1/2 TURN

17	18	19	&	20
Step R Forward	1/2 Turn L; Step L Forward	Step R Forward	Step L Together	Step R Forward

21	22	23	24
Step L Forward	1/2 Turn R; Step R Forward	Step L Forward	Step R Back; Rock Back

ROCK AND CHA-CHA

25	26	27	&	28
Step L Forward; Rock Forward	Step R Back; Rock Back	Step L Forward	Step R Together	Step L Forward

Romeo

Choreographed for the song "Romeo" by Dolly Parton, this dance is light and lively. It includes some syncopated steps that will make you feel like you are tap dancing!

Music Suggestion

"Romeo" by Dolly Parton

Step Descriptions

1-4   Step R forward, brush L, lift L knee and one-quarter turn L, step back L, stomp R

5-8   One-quarter turn R and big step R pushing hips to L, big step L pushing hips to R, step R closer to L pushing hips to L, step L closer to R pushing hips R

9-12   Grapevine R (step R to R, step L behind R, step R to R), drag L next to R and lift knee

13-16   Step L to L and one-quarter turn L, continue to turn L another one-quarter turn and drop heel on count 14, continue to turn L another one-quarter turn and drop heel on count 15, continue turning until facing original wall and stomp R

17&   Tap L forward, bring L together, tap
18&   R forward, bring R together

19&   Tap L behind R, bring L together

20&21   Tap R behind L, bring R together, tap L to L side turning toe in

&22&   Bring L together, tap R toe to R side turning toe in, one-quarter turn L and step R next to L

23&24   Tap L heel forward, step L to L, tap R toe back

25-28   Putting weight on ball of R, roll hips to R, shift weight to L and roll hips to L, shift weight to ball of R and roll hips to R, shift weight to L foot and roll hips to L

29-32   Shift weight to ball of R and circle hips to R, shift weight to ball of L and continue hip circle, shift weight to ball of R and circle hips again to R, drop R heel and shift weight L and complete hip roll

Foot Map

FORWARD AND BRUSH

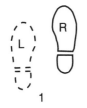 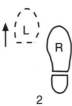

1	2	&	3	4
Step R Forward	Brush L	Lift L Knee and 1/4 Turn L	Step L Back	Stomp R

(continued)

ROMEO (continued)

HIPS

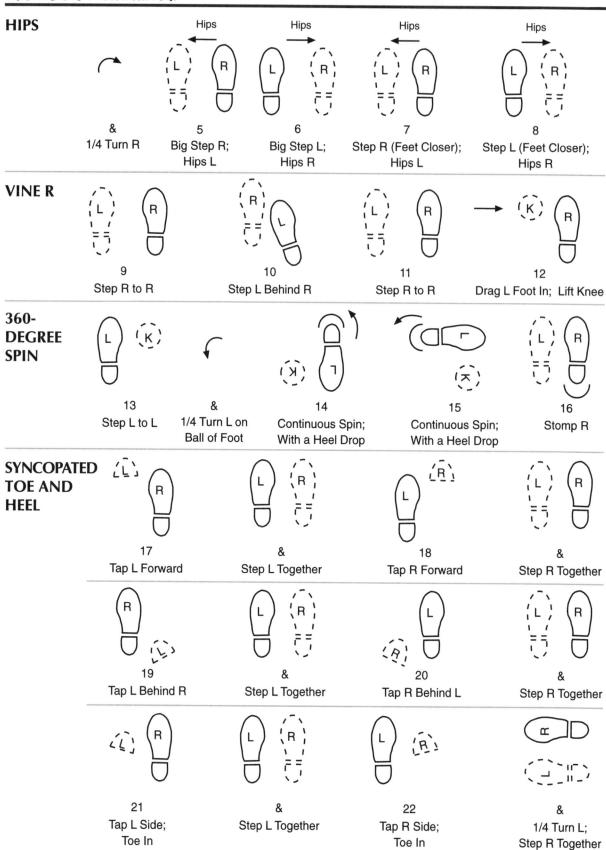

&	5	6	7	8
1/4 Turn R	Big Step R; Hips L	Big Step L; Hips R	Step R (Feet Closer); Hips L	Step L (Feet Closer); Hips R

VINE R

9	10	11	12
Step R to R	Step L Behind R	Step R to R	Drag L Foot In; Lift Knee

360-DEGREE SPIN

13	&	14	15	16
Step L to L	1/4 Turn L on Ball of Foot	Continuous Spin; With a Heel Drop	Continuous Spin; With a Heel Drop	Stomp R

SYNCOPATED TOE AND HEEL

17	&	18	&
Tap L Forward	Step L Together	Tap R Forward	Step R Together

19	&	20	&
Tap L Behind R	Step L Together	Tap R Behind L	Step R Together

21	&	22	&
Tap L Side; Toe In	Step L Together	Tap R Side; Toe In	1/4 Turn L; Step R Together

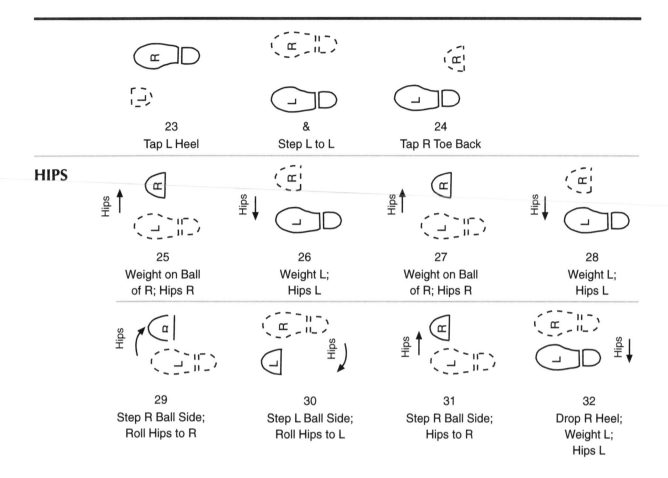

23	&	24
Tap L Heel	Step L to L	Tap R Toe Back

HIPS

25	26	27	28
Weight on Ball of R; Hips R	Weight L; Hips L	Weight on Ball of R; Hips R	Weight L; Hips L

29	30	31	32
Step R Ball Side; Roll Hips to R	Step L Ball Side; Roll Hips to L	Step R Ball Side; Hips to R	Drop R Heel; Weight L; Hips L

Brush

Achy Breaky

This dance was choreographed to the song "Achy Breaky Heart" by Billy Ray Cyrus. Many feel that this song renewed line dancing and started the craze in the 1990s. The three-quarter turn into a walk backwards is what makes this dance a challenge.

Music Suggestions

"Achy Breaky Heart" by Billy Ray Cyrus

"Some Kind of Trouble" by Tanya Tucker

"Home Sweet Home" by Dennis Robbins

Step Descriptions

1-4	Grapevine R (step R to R, cross L behind R, step R to R), hold
5-8	Bump hips L, bump hips R, bump hips L, hold one beat with hips to L
9-12	Touch R toe back, tap R toe to R, step R toe forward and push one-quarter turn L, continue turning one-half turn L on ball of L foot, step back on R (three-quarter turn when completed)
13-16	Walk back L, R, raise L knee and one-quarter turn L, step L together

17-20	Walk back R, L, R, stomp L next to R
21-24	Bump hips L, bump hips R, bump hips L, hold one beat with hip to L
25-28	One-quarter turn R and step R to R, stomp L foot next to R, one-half turn L and step L to L, stomp R next to L
29-32	Grapevine R (step R to R, cross L behind R, step R to R), stomp L next to R and shift weight to L

Variation

Substitute single or double rolling grapevines for any of the grapevines.

Foot Map

VINE R

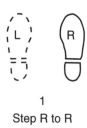
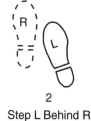

1	2	3	4
Step R to R	Step L Behind R	Step R to R	Hold

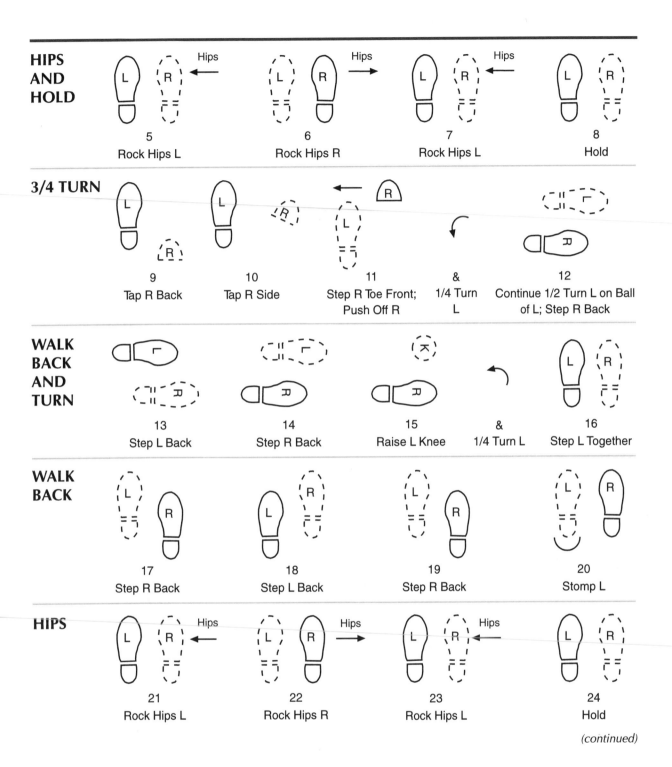

HIPS AND HOLD

5	6	7	8
Rock Hips L	Rock Hips R	Rock Hips L	Hold

3/4 TURN

9	10	11	&	12
Tap R Back	Tap R Side	Step R Toe Front; Push Off R	1/4 Turn L	Continue 1/2 Turn L on Ball of L; Step R Back

WALK BACK AND TURN

13	14	15	&	16
Step L Back	Step R Back	Raise L Knee	1/4 Turn L	Step L Together

WALK BACK

17	18	19	20
Step R Back	Step L Back	Step R Back	Stomp L

HIPS

21	22	23	24
Rock Hips L	Rock Hips R	Rock Hips L	Hold

(continued)

167

Achy Breaky (continued)

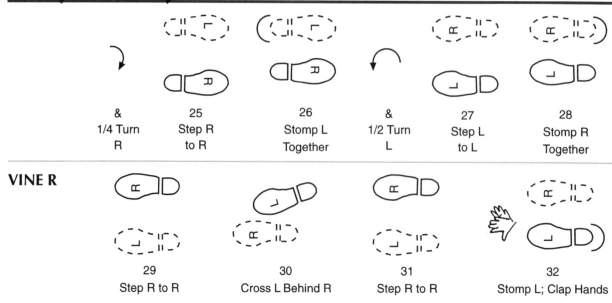

& 1/4 Turn R	25 Step R to R	26 Stomp L Together	& 1/2 Turn L	27 Step L to L	28 Stomp R Together

VINE R

29 Step R to R	30 Cross L Behind R	31 Step R to R	32 Stomp L; Clap Hands

Hip Bump

Hips move L.   Hips move R.

LeDoux Shuffle

This dance is listed as an advanced-level dance only because of its length. If performed slowly, this could be considered an intermediate-level dance. For fun, try using as much floor space as possible on the shuffles.

Music Suggestions

"Cadillac Ranch" by Chris LeDoux

"Honky Tonk Crowd" by Rick Trevino

"Born to Boogie" by Hank Williams, Jr.

Step Descriptions

1-4	Tap R heel forward, cross R over L and tap R toe, tap R heel forward, bring R together
5-8	Tap L heel forward, cross L over R and tap L toe, tap L heel forward, bring L together
9-12	Repeat counts 1-4
13-16	Shuffle forward R (step R forward, step L together, step R forward), step L forward, shift weight back on R
17-20	Shuffle back L (step L back, step R together, step L back), step R back, shift weight forward on L
21-24	Shuffle forward R (step R forward, step L together, step R forward), step L forward, pivot turn R and step R forward
25-28	Shuffle forward L (step L forward, step R together, step L forward), step R forward, one-quarter turn L and step L forward
29-32	Step R forward, pivot turn L and step L forward, stomp R, hold and clap hands
33-36	Tap R toe four times
37-40	Switch feet and tap L toe four times
41-44	Tap R heel forward, switch feet and tap L heel forward, switch feet and tap R heel forward, hold and clap
45-48	Place R foot down and bump hips forward twice, shift weight to L and bump hips back twice

49-52	Bump hips forward, bump hips back, bump hips forward, bump hips back continually shifting weight
53-56	Shuffle forward R, step L forward, shift weight back on R
57-60	Shuffle back L, step R back, shift weight forward on L
61&62	Shuffle forward R
63-66	Step L forward, pivot turn R and step R forward, shuffle forward L
67-70	Step R forward, one-quarter turn L and step L forward, step R forward, pivot turn L, step L forward
71-74	Stomp R beside L, jump both feet apart, jump together with R crossed over L, one-half turn L and jump feet together
75-78	Shuffle forward R, step L forward, shift weight back on R
79-82	Shuffle back L, step R back, shift weight forward on L
83-86	Shuffle forward R, step L forward, pivot turn R and step R forward
87&88	Shuffle forward L
89-92	Step R forward, one-quarter turn L and step L forward, step R forward, pivot turn L and step L forward
93-96	Cross R over L, step L back, step R to R, stomp L together ending with weight on L

LeDoux Shuffle (continued)

Foot Map

HEEL, TOE

1	2	3	4
R Heel Forward	Cross R Toe Over L	R Heel Forward	Together

5	6	7	8
L Heel Forward	Cross L Toe Over R	L Heel Forward	Together

9	10	11	12
R Heel Forward	Cross R Toe Over L	R Heel Forward	Together

SHUFFLE FORWARD

13	&	14	15	16
Step R Forward	Step L Together	Step R Forward	Step L Forward	Weight Back on R

SHUFFLE BACK

17	&	18	19	20
Step L Back	Step R Together	Step L Back	Step R Back	Weight Forward on L

SHUFFLE WITH 1/2 TURN

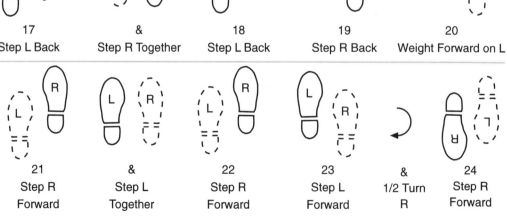

21	&	22	23	&	24
Step R Forward	Step L Together	Step R Forward	Step L Forward	1/2 Turn R	Step R Forward

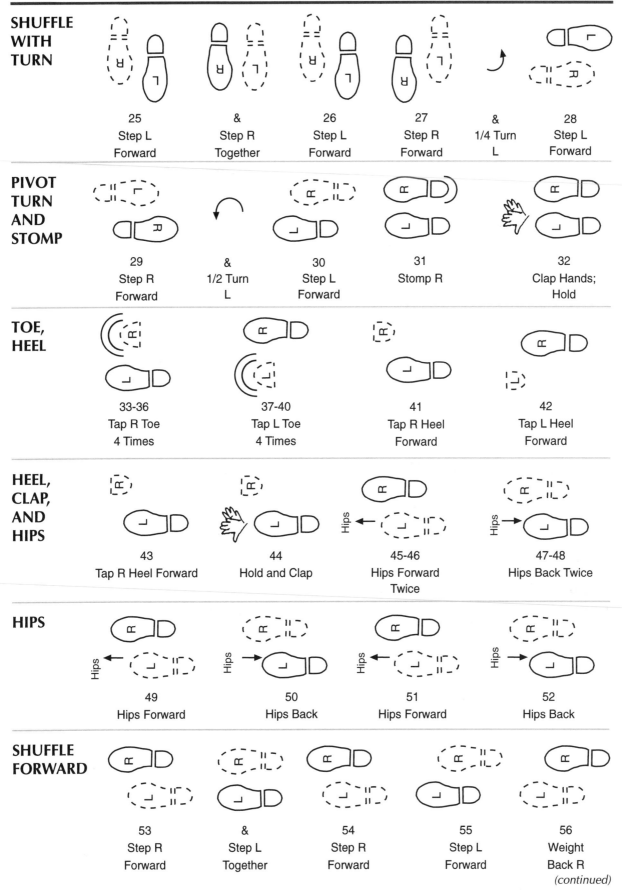

SHUFFLE WITH TURN

25	&	26	27	&	28
Step L Forward	Step R Together	Step L Forward	Step R Forward	1/4 Turn L	Step L Forward

PIVOT TURN AND STOMP

29	&	30	31	32
Step R Forward	1/2 Turn L	Step L Forward	Stomp R	Clap Hands; Hold

TOE, HEEL

33-36	37-40	41	42
Tap R Toe 4 Times	Tap L Toe 4 Times	Tap R Heel Forward	Tap L Heel Forward

HEEL, CLAP, AND HIPS

43	44	45-46	47-48
Tap R Heel Forward	Hold and Clap	Hips Forward Twice	Hips Back Twice

HIPS

49	50	51	52
Hips Forward	Hips Back	Hips Forward	Hips Back

SHUFFLE FORWARD

53	&	54	55	56
Step R Forward	Step L Together	Step R Forward	Step L Forward	Weight Back R

(continued)

LeDoux Shuffle (continued)

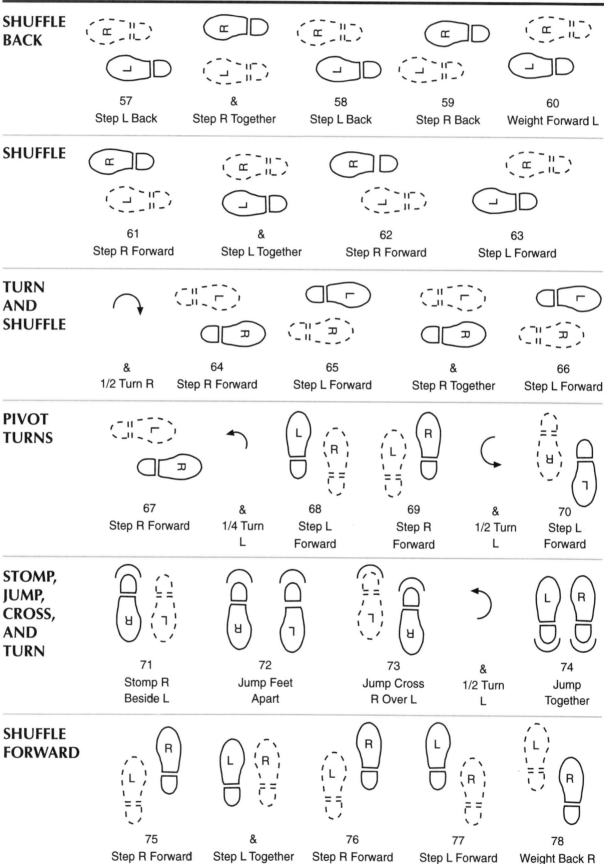

SHUFFLE BACK

57	&	58	59	60
Step L Back	Step R Together	Step L Back	Step R Back	Weight Forward L

SHUFFLE

61	&	62	63
Step R Forward	Step L Together	Step R Forward	Step L Forward

TURN AND SHUFFLE

&	64	65	&	66
1/2 Turn R	Step R Forward	Step L Forward	Step R Together	Step L Forward

PIVOT TURNS

67	&	68	69	&	70
Step R Forward	1/4 Turn L	Step L Forward	Step R Forward	1/2 Turn L	Step L Forward

STOMP, JUMP, CROSS, AND TURN

71	72	73	&	74
Stomp R Beside L	Jump Feet Apart	Jump Cross R Over L	1/2 Turn L	Jump Together

SHUFFLE FORWARD

75	&	76	77	78
Step R Forward	Step L Together	Step R Forward	Step L Forward	Weight Back R

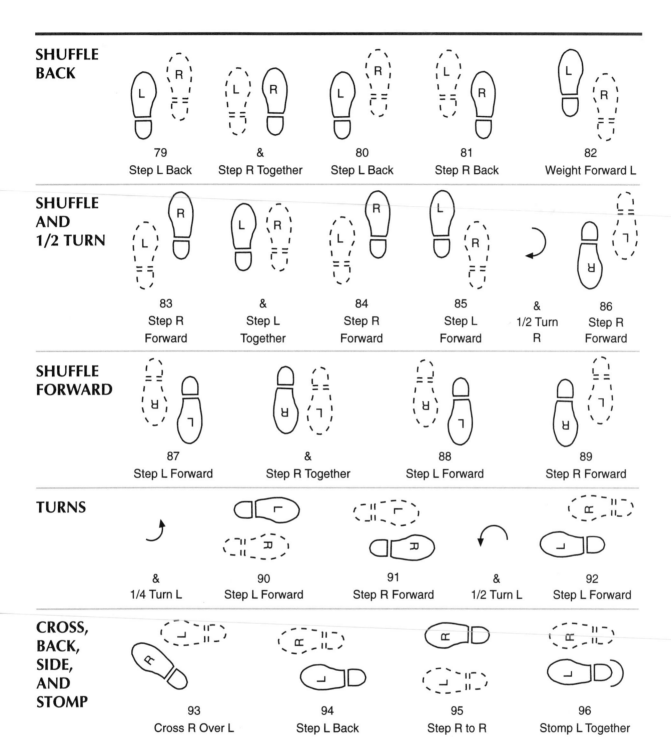

SHUFFLE BACK

79	&	80	81	82
Step L Back	Step R Together	Step L Back	Step R Back	Weight Forward L

SHUFFLE AND 1/2 TURN

83	&	84	85	&	86
Step R Forward	Step L Together	Step R Forward	Step L Forward	1/2 Turn R	Step R Forward

SHUFFLE FORWARD

87	&	88	89
Step L Forward	Step R Together	Step L Forward	Step R Forward

TURNS

&	90	91	&	92
1/4 Turn L	Step L Forward	Step R Forward	1/2 Turn L	Step L Forward

CROSS, BACK, SIDE, AND STOMP

93	94	95	96
Cross R Over L	Step L Back	Step R to R	Stomp L Together

Hip-Hop

This dance is definitely an aerobic workout! Besides these suggested songs, try this dance to the current funky songs on the charts today with a rhythm of about 120 BPM.

Music Suggestions

"Funky Cowboy" by Ronnie McDowell

"I'm Cowboy" by Smokin' Armadillos

"Put Some Drive in Your Country" by Travis Tritt

Step Descriptions

1-4	(Paddle Turn) Step with L four times making one-quarter turn to R
5-8	(Paddle Turn) Step with R four times making one-quarter turn to L
9&10&	Jump feet apart, feet together, feet apart, feet together (Jumping Jacks)
11& 12&	One-half turn R as jump feet apart, feet together, feet apart, feet together
13& 14&	One-half turn L as jump feet apart, feet together, feet apart, feet together
15&16	One-half turn R as jump feet apart, feet together, feet apart
17-20	(Paddle Turn) Step with R four times making one-quarter turn to L
21& 22&	Kick L forward, step L back, step R back, step L forward
23&24	Scuff R forward, one-quarter turn L and lift R knee, stomp R ending with weight on R
25-40	Repeat counts 21-24 four more times
41-43	Step L to L, cross R behind L, step L in place, step R to R
44&45	Cross L behind R, step R in place, step L to L
46-48	Cross R behind L, step L in place, step R to R, step L to L
49-52	Step R and slide R back, step L and slide L back, step R and slide R back (Running Man), swivel R, return heels to center
53-56	Step L and slide L back, step R and slide R back, step L and slide L back (Running Man), swivel heels L, return heels to center

57-60	Jump feet apart, jump and end crossing R over L, jump feet apart, jump together, jump feet apart
61-64	Jump both feet together traveling R, jump both feet together traveling L, jump both feet together traveling R three times
65-68	Scissor splits out and in, scissor splits out, in, out traveling L
69-72	One-quarter turn R, step R to R and pull arms back, one-half turn L, step L to L and pull back arms, one-half turn R, step R to R and pull back arms, step L together and clap
73-76	One-half turn L, step L and touch R to R, one-half turn R, step R to R, one-half turn L, step L and touch R to R, jump crossing L in front of R, jump feet apart
77-80	Pick up R and one-half turn R, step L and touch R to R, one-half turn L, step R to R, pick up R and one-half turn R, step R to R, jump crossing R in front of L, step R together, one-quarter turn L
81-84	Big step forward on L for two counts, step R together and hold
85-88	Big step back on R for two counts, step L together and hold
89-90	Jump back on R and kick L, jump L forward, jump R forward, jump L back (Electric Kick)
91-92	Repeat counts 89-90
93-96	Step L back, step R forward, one-quarter turn L, step L forward, step R together keeping weight on R, and clap

Foot Map

PADDLE TURN R

1   2   3   4

Step L Four Times Doing 1/4 Turn R (Paddle Turn R)

PADDLE TURN L

5   6   7   8

Step R Four Times Doing 1/4 Turn L (Paddle Turn L)

JUMPS

9	&	10	&
Jump Out	Jump Together	Jump Out	Jump Together

TURN AND JUMP

11	&	12	&
1/2 Turn R and Jump Out	Jump Together	Jump Out	Jump Together

13	&	14	&
1/2 Turn L and Jump Out	Jump Together	Jump Out	Jump Together

15	&	16
1/2 Turn R and Jump Out	Jump Together	Jump Out

(continued)

PADDLE TURN

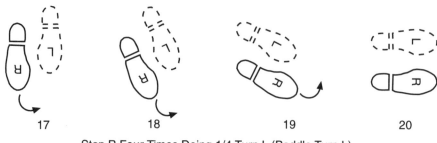

17   18   19   20

Step R Four Times Doing 1/4 Turn L (Paddle Turn L)

FUNKY KICK

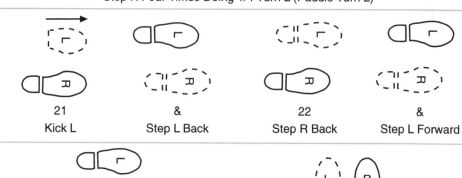

| 21 | & | 22 | & |
| Kick L | Step L Back | Step R Back | Step L Forward |

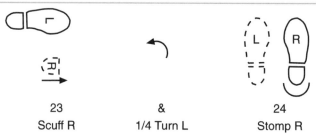

| 23 | & | 24 |
| Scuff R | 1/4 Turn L | Stomp R |

25-40

Repeat funky kick four more times; end facing front.

SAILOR STEP

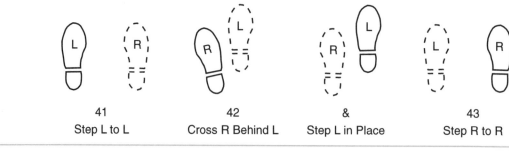

| 41 | 42 | & | 43 |
| Step L to L | Cross R Behind L | Step L in Place | Step R to R |

| 44 | & | 45 |
| Cross L Behind R | Step R in Place | Step L to L |

176

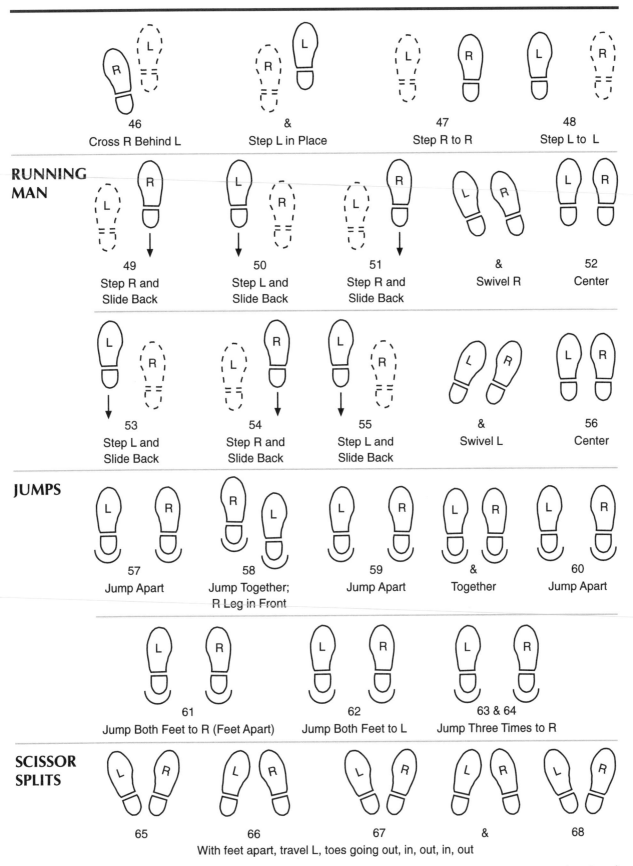

	46	&	47	48
	Cross R Behind L	Step L in Place	Step R to R	Step L to L

RUNNING MAN

49	50	51	&	52
Step R and Slide Back	Step L and Slide Back	Step R and Slide Back	Swivel R	Center

53	54	55	&	56
Step L and Slide Back	Step R and Slide Back	Step L and Slide Back	Swivel L	Center

JUMPS

57	58	59	&	60
Jump Apart	Jump Together; R Leg in Front	Jump Apart	Together	Jump Apart

61	62	63 & 64
Jump Both Feet to R (Feet Apart)	Jump Both Feet to L	Jump Three Times to R

SCISSOR SPLITS

65	66	67	&	68

With feet apart, travel L, toes going out, in, out, in, out

(continued)

Hip-Hop (continued)

PULL BACKS

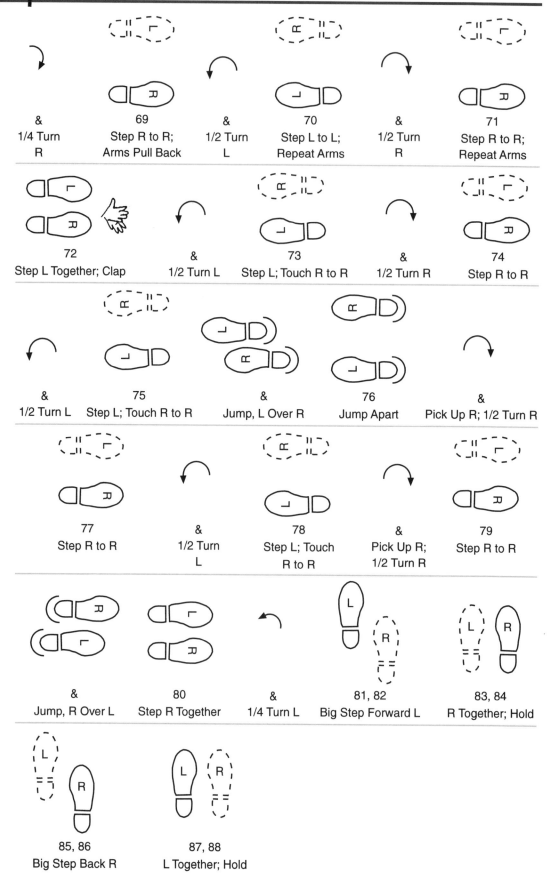

&	69	&	70	&	71
1/4 Turn R	Step R to R; Arms Pull Back	1/2 Turn L	Step L to L; Repeat Arms	1/2 Turn R	Step R to R; Repeat Arms

72	&	73	&	74
Step L Together; Clap	1/2 Turn L	Step L; Touch R to R	1/2 Turn R	Step R to R

&	75	&	76	&
1/2 Turn L	Step L; Touch R to R	Jump, L Over R	Jump Apart	Pick Up R; 1/2 Turn R

77	&	78	&	79
Step R to R	1/2 Turn L	Step L; Touch R to R	Pick Up R; 1/2 Turn R	Step R to R

&	80	&	81, 82	83, 84
Jump, R Over L	Step R Together	1/4 Turn L	Big Step Forward L	R Together; Hold

85, 86	87, 88
Big Step Back R	L Together; Hold

ELECTRIC KICK

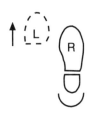   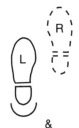

89	&	90	&
Jump Back R; Kick L	Jump L Forward	Jump R Forward	Jump L Back

  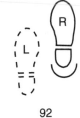 

91	&	92	&
Jump Back R; Kick L	Jump L Forward	Jump R Forward	Jump L Back

STEP AND TURN

93	&	94	95, 96
Step R Forward	1/4 Turn L or 1 1/4 Turn L	Step L Forward	Step R Together; Clap

Jump R back, kick L.   Jump L forward.   Jump R forward.   Jump L back.

Here's a challenge that is also fun. This dance is actually four line dances performed together. First, you perform the Cowboy Boogie once and then immediately do the Honky Tonk Stomp. After you perform the Honky Tonk Stomp once, dance the Electric Slide I. Perform the Electric Slide I once and then add on the Smooth. After you perform all these dances together, repeat from the top and you will feel like you can conquer the world!

Music Suggestions

"Gone Country" by Alan Jackson

"Achy Breaky Heart" by Billy Ray Cyrus

"Honky Tonk Attitude" by Joe Diffie

Step Descriptions

Add the following dances together:

Cowboy Boogie (see page 25)

Honky Tonk Stomp (see page 69)

Electric Slide I (see page 27)

Smooth (see page 36)

Share the Fun With Others!

Partner-Pattern Dances

Now that you have mastered the line dances and are feeling confident (I said confident, not cocky), it is time to try something new. This chapter presents several line dances that you can do with a partner. For example, you will get a chance to try the Barn Dance Mixer. During this dance you will have an opportunity to change partners. It's a great way to liven up a party!

In partner-pattern dancing, couples perform the same patterned foot movements, holding on to each other in selected arm positions. They travel in the line of dance repeating the sequence until the music ends. Sounds fun, huh?

The arm positions for the following dances are the sweetheart position, also known as the side-by-side position; the modified-sweetheart position, also known as the dancing skaters' position; the double-handhold or "open" position; and the country-western "closed" position. In the sweetheart position, the couple faces the line of dance joining hands. The woman is on the man's right side. The partners hold right hands slightly in front of the woman's right shoulder and left hands slightly in front of the man's left shoulder (see page 183). The modified-sweetheart position is similar to the sweetheart position, except that the woman is slightly in front of the man's right hip and the right hands rest on the woman's right hip. The partners join left hands in front of the man at chest level (see page 183). In the double-handhold position the couple faces each other while holding hands, with the woman's hands on top and her fingers in the man's palms (see page 184). The couple also faces each other in the country-western closed position, but the man holds the woman's right hand in his left at shoulder height (see page 184). His right hand is on her upper-left back, while the woman's left hand rests on the man's upper-right arm. Sometimes dances performed in the open position are also danced in the closed position.

Note that in all dances in this chapter, men and women do the same footwork, unless specified otherwise. Well, that's it. You already know the basic steps and terminology, so let's do it!

Barn Dance Mixer	185	Ten-Step	183
Cotton-Eyed Joe	184	Traveling Cha-Cha	186

This is called the Ten-Step because that is exactly what you need to learn—ten steps before you shuffle! This dance is similar to the Cotton-Eyed Joe because it is performed in a circle, has shuffles, and can be done with groups as well as partners.

Performed in the line of dance with partners in the sweetheart position.

Music Suggestions

"Liza Jane" by Vince Gill

"God Bless Texas" by Little Texas

"Men" by the Forester Sisters

Step Descriptions

Men and ladies perform the same footwork.

1-4	Tap L heel forward, step L next to R, tap R toe back, step R next to L
5-8	Tap R heel forward, hitch R, tap R heel forward, step R next to L
9-10	Tap L heel forward, hitch L

11&12	Shuffle forward L (step L forward, step R together, step L forward)
13&14	Shuffle forward R (step R forward, step L together, step R forward)
15&16	Shuffle forward L
17&18	Shuffle forward R

Variations

1. During the shuffle steps (counts 11-18) partners can try to switch sides. Or the lady can go under the man's arm during the shuffles.

2. Create a mixer! See variation 2 for Cotton-Eyed Joe, page 184.

Sweetheart position.

Modified-sweetheart position.

Cotton-Eyed Joe

At one time, this dance was done as a tradition at many clubs close to the end of the evening. It may be danced not only with two people but with three or four side-by-side holding hands or putting arms around waists.

Performed in a circle facing the line of dance with partners in the sweetheart position.

Music Suggestions

"Cotton Eyed Joe" by the Rednex

"Cotton Eyed Joe" by Isaac Payton Sweat

"Cotton Eyed Joe" on *Christy Lane Party Dance Music*

Step Descriptions

Men and ladies perform the same footwork.

1-4   Stomp or hook L, kick L, shuffle back L (step L back, step R together, step L back)

5-8   Stomp or hook R, kick R, shuffle back R (step R back, step L together, step R back)

9-12   Repeat counts 1-4

13-16   Repeat counts 5-8

17&18   Shuffle forward L (step L forward, step R together, step L forward)

19&20   Shuffle forward R (step R forward, step L together, step R forward)

21-32   Repeat counts 17-20 three more times

Variations

1. Try various turns while performing the shuffles in counts 17 to 32.

2. Create a mixer where you can change partners during counts 17 to 32. The lady travels forward to the next man while the man shuffles in place waiting for the lady behind him.

Double-handhold position.

Country-western closed position.

Barn Dance Mixer

This dance will be a standard as long as there is country line dancing. It is performed in a circle with men on the inside and women on the outside facing the line of dance. Partners begin by facing each other, and this becomes a mixer when the women take a new partner coming from the left after count 28, and men take a new partner coming from their left after the same count.

Performed in a circle in the line of dance with partners facing each other in a double-handhold position. This can also be done in a closed position.

Music Suggestions

"Walkin' After Midnight" by Garth Brooks

"Dumas Walker" by Kentucky Headhunters

"Wild Wild West" by the Escape Club

Step Descriptions

Men

1-4	Step L to L, step R together, step L to L, tap R
5-8	Step R to R, step L together, step R to R, tap L
9-12	Step L to L, step R together, step L to L, tap R
13-16	Step R to R, step L together, step R to R, tap L
17-20	(Face LOD) Step L, hop on L, step R, hop on R
21-24	Step L, hop on L, step R, hop on R
25-28	Face LOD and grapevine L (step L to L, cross R behind L, step L to L, tap R)
29-32	Grapevine R (step R to R, cross L behind R, step R to R) and one-quarter turn R to face partner

Ladies

1-4	Step R to R, step L together, step R to R, tap L
5-8	Step L to L, step R together, step L to L, tap R
9-12	Three-step turn R (R, L, R)
13-16	Three-step turn L (L, R, L)
17-20	(Face LOD) Step R, hop on R, step L, hop on L
21-24	Step R, hop on R, step L, hop on L
25-28	Face LOD and grapevine R (step R to R, cross L behind R, step R to R, tap L)
29-32	Grapevine L (step L to L, cross R behind L, step L to L) and one-quarter turn L to face partner

Variations

1. Replace counts 18, 20, 22, and 24 with a hitch instead of a hop.

2. Repeat counts 25 to 32 at the end of the dance to make the dance 40 counts long.

3. On counts 29 to 32, replace with a three-step turn and end facing a new partner.

Traveling Cha-Cha

This dance has also been called the Cowboy Cha-Cha. It can be done in place or by traveling in the line of dance. Cha-cha rhythms seem to have come from our Latin American neighbors who are known for music that drives souls crazy. Any cha-cha music will work for this romantic dance.

Performed in the line of dance with partners in the sweetheart position.

Music Suggestions

"Neon Moon" by Brooks and Dunn

"Gulf of Mexico" by Clint Black

"Love Is Still Alive" by Midnight Rodeo

Step Descriptions

Note: All steps are performed in a cha-cha rhythm (1-2, 3&4).

Men and Ladies

1-4   Step L forward, step R back, step L back, step R together, step L back

5-8   Step R back, step L forward, step R forward, step L together, step R forward

9-12   Step L forward, step R back, step L back, step R together, step L back

Men

13-28   Repeat counts 5-12 twice

Ladies

13-16   Step R back, step L forward, step R as begin one-half turn L, step L back as turn L, step R back

17-20   Step L back, step R forward, step L as begin one-half turn R, step R back, step L back

21-28   Repeat counts 13-20.

Men and Ladies

29-32   Step R in place, step L in place, step R in place, put weight on L, put weight on R

33-36   Step L forward, one-half turn R, step R forward, step L forward, step R together, step L forward

37-40   Step R forward, one-half turn L, step L forward, step R forward, step L together, step R forward

49-52   Step L forward, step R forward, step L forward, step R together, step L forward

53-56   Step R forward, step L forward, step R forward, step L together, step R forward

Men

73-76   Cross L behind R, step R to R, step L forward, step R to R, step L to L

77-80   Step R back, step L together, step R in place, step L in place, step R in place

Ladies

73-76   Step L forward, cross R over L, step L back, step R to R, cross L over R

77-80   Step R to R, step L forward, one-half turn R, step R forward, one-quarter turn R and step L forward, one-quarter turn R and step R forward

Men and Ladies

81-88   Repeat counts 73-80

Developing Technique and Style

Alright! We are now ready to shine. Here are some pointers to give you extra special flair on the dance floor.

Technique

A common dance style today is to use a country-western technique. Although you will find some differences throughout the country, the usual technique is to carry your weight over the ball of the foot. Take small steps, as this will make you more agile and mobile. As your dancing improves, you can start taking longer steps, if desired. As you walk forward, step with a heel-ball-toe action with your feet close to the floor. When stepping backward, move from the hips, again keeping your feet close to the floor, with the heel reaching back to gain full extension on each step. Keep the knees bent, not flexed, as straight legs take away from smoothness and grace in dancing. Remember, as mentioned in chapter 1, good posture and arm control will aid in good technique.

The ideal country-western dancer is smooth, so try not to bounce. Try keeping your upper torso quiet, with your shoulders relaxed, as your lower body does all the work gliding across the floor. Over the years, line dancers have become more free with their bodies. For example, a "funky" dancer picks up the feet and uses the upper body, letting the rib cage, shoulders, and head move as much as possible while freestyling with the arms. Buy yourself a video camera and watch yourself dance. It is an excellent training aid.

Style

After you learn the basic pattern of a dance, work on doing it more smoothly and with unique styling. The number of dances, patterns, turns, and movements is almost unlimited, but don't fall into the trap of learning steps rather than dancing. Style is the essence of creativity. It is the personal expression given to dance through your body carriage and feeling. It allows freedom for individual interpretation and improvisation. By putting your individual interpretation into the steps, you create your own style. One way to assist you in developing your style is to try this small exercise (what I call "play"). The next time you practice dancing, turn on the music and permit your body to move freely to the beat. Try to capture the essence of your body moving with no limitations. Do whatever comes naturally—nothing is right or wrong.

Having trouble moving freely? One way to help your body feel the music is through isolation exercises. By practicing movement of different parts of your body, you become more conscious of how your entire body moves. For example, let's focus on the hip movements used in dances such as the Tush Push. Stand center, facing forward with your feet apart. Bend your knees and move your hips to the right and left. Repeat slowly and continuously, then increase the speed of the isolated hip movements. Do the same thing while moving your hips forward and back; then forward, side, back, side; and then reverse these movements. Finish by rolling your hips in each direction.

If you want to try line dances with a funky flair, practice isolating the rib cage the same way you isolated your hips. Stand, facing forward with your feet apart, and move the rib cage side to side (this is going to feel very strange!). Next move your rib cage front and back, and then move it front and back while dancing the grapevine. This definitely makes your line dancing look "funky."

Are you holding your head stiff as a board while you dance? Try dancing the grapevine to the right and left, and relax the head by nodding it up and down slightly while you move. (It helps to get the rhythm flowing through your body if you nod while dancing, as if saying, "Yes!") Now, continue doing the grapevine, only this time concentrate on your shoulders. Move them any way you want—up, down, forward, back—or shake them side to side. Sometimes even just thinking about relaxing your shoulders helps your body move more smoothly.

Now that you have tried isolating different parts of the body, practice performing various line dances and be attentive to what the different parts of your body do as you dance. Try to move your hips, head, and rib cage all at the same time. Your awareness and coordination will increase with every part of the body that you integrate into your steps. Let the music flow through your body as it moves naturally. And there it is— your style!

Variations

One way to spice up your dancing is with variations, such as fancy turns and spins. For example, whenever a grapevine is called for in a line dance, replace it with a turn. Here are some techniques that will help you with turns:

1. *Maintain good posture.* It is essential in dance and is a tremendous source of control when turning. If your body falls out of alignment even slightly, the force of turning will throw you off balance.

2. *Control your arms.* Don't just let them hang. Use your shoulders to help you rotate. For example, when turning to the right, pull your shoulder to the right, being careful to maintain proper alignment.

3. *Focus with your eyes.* There is a technique in dance to keep you from getting dizzy. It is called "spotting." Try focusing your eyes on an object at eye level after you have finished turning. Then try executing multiple turns in the same amount of time that you would take to make one turn, each time focusing your eyes on the object or "spot." Multiple turns are both challenging and fun.

4. *Practice your timing.* Timing in turns is developed through consistent practice. Notice the difference in feeling when you perform two turns as compared to three or four. Speed will be greater as you increase the number of turns. You will need to find your own timing. Try to practice turning at different tempos and speeds.

Another variation is to double-time your movements to single-time rhythm. Let's use a heel split as an example. If the dance calls for one heel split to be performed in two counts, a variation would be to perform two heel splits also in two counts. Your count would be "&1&2" as opposed to "1, 2" and your feet would go out, in, out, in as opposed to just out and in. There are unlimited possibilities in double-timing steps, as long as you do it in the same amount of time as the original step, so that you end up on the same count as the other dancers on the floor.

You can always substitute steps as variations, as long as you don't interfere with other dancers. That is what is so great about line dancing—it has unlimited possibilities.

So the next time you do recreational dancing, remember, anything goes. Feel the music—let it get into your soul—and see what type of choreography you can create!

Attitude

Have you ever noticed how negative emotions, like nervous tension, anxiety, or low self-esteem, can affect your dancing? It is amazing just how much the mind can control the body. Dance has many similarities to athletics. Just like an athlete, a dancer must practice mental, as well as physical, training. Mental training can help you get rid of psychological barriers.

Visualize yourself having confidence and dancing the way you want to dance. Believe in yourself and mentally see yourself accomplishing your goals. Then watch how it shows in your style on the dance floor. Confidence can be learned, and nothing can stop you from attaining it.

So here's an experiment. The next time you feel a little bit inhibited or anxious when you dance, channel your emotional anxiety and become aware of your body and mind by tuning into your feelings and emotions. Relax both mind and body by letting go and breathing deeply and easily. Breathing into the abdomen is one of the most valuable techniques for focusing, calming, and energizing yourself. Remain focused on your dancing in a positive way and always visualize yourself making the dance moves you desire. Be adventurous and try adding more movements with your hips or ribs, or try performing a double-kick where there is a single-kick. Tell your mind to tell your body!

Was there ever a time when everything seemed to flow? Remember the harmony of your body and mind and how it felt? This is the state you want to reach—when you commit every aspect of yourself to the movement. Mental rehearsal is very important if you want to perform well, so practice mentally as well as physically. It will show on the dance floor.

For Teachers Only

You do not have to be a great dancer to be a great teacher. In fact, the trained dancer has an advantage over someone who is a "natural dancer" because the trained dancer can relate better to skill development and student needs. One thing is certain—to be a good educator, you must have a keen desire to help others.

Use this checklist if you are interested in becoming a line dance instructor. Put a check by each area in which you feel qualified.

- ❏ Desire to help others
- ❏ Good communication skills
- ❏ Knowledge of the subject
- ❏ Good organization skills
- ❏ Proper facility, equipment, and attire
- ❏ Good self-esteem and confidence level

If you have checked off every quality but are not currently instructing, give it a try. Teaching dance can be hard work, but there is no better reward than helping others. If you checked off only a few of the qualities, there is always time to develop the others if you truly wish to teach. Assuming you may want to teach, let's talk about how to put together the ingredients of a good line dance class.

Facility

First, you need a facility. Before you get too excited and build a brand new building to teach your line dancing classes, consider establishing a following of students. Teaching part-time in an already established facility, such as a nightclub, dance studio, or school gymnasium, is a great way to get started. Nightclub owners are always looking for ways to bring more people into their places of business, so classes offered before the evening crowd arrives may prove to be your best bet. You can work on a commission or salary. However, be aware that in a nightclub you may have to deal with people who smoke or use alcohol. So if that is not your desire, you may prefer employment by a local community center, YMCA, YWCA, recreation department, Boys or Girls Club, senior center, health club, dance studio, church, or continuing education program.

A dance studio is a great place for line dance instruction for three reasons: people go there strictly to dance, it has mirrors, and it offers a professional environment. But a disadvantage of instructing at a private dance studio is that you will be competing against other classes for space in the prime-time slots. Of course, any building large enough to accommodate the number of dancers you wish to teach at one time would work. Just try to avoid rooms with beams (so you don't have to worry about bumping into them).

Be aware of floor friction when choosing a surface for dancing. Wood or tile floors are the best surfaces for dancing. Be careful of a rubber floor called marlee, which is popular in the dance studios that offer ballet. This type of rubber surface makes turning and sliding difficult, which can be dangerous to the ankles and knees. In fact, rubber flooring of any type can be a hindrance to a line dancer because of the need to slide, glide, and turn easily. If you are planning on teaching at a recreation center, school facility, or health club, be aware that many of the floors in these locations are made for tennis shoes rather than cowboy boots. Advise your students to pick up their feet as they turn and slide in these types of facilities. And, if possible, try to avoid a carpeted floor.

Be sure the acoustics are clear. Echoes are very frustrating for participants trying to hear the beat. You can try to reduce the echo in the room by adjusting the treble and bass on your sound system. But if you have no choice and are in a room with poor acoustics, a higher quality sound system—especially a more powerful amplifier and speakers—may solve the problem.

Proper ventilation and circulation are always helpful. However, if you live in a comfortable outdoor environment, like the Hawaiian Islands, dancing outside is a marvelous experience. (Line dancing under a palm tree does wonders for the soul!) Be sure restrooms and drinking water are readily available. (Remember, soft drinks and alcohol can dehydrate your students, making them feel tired.)

If you are employed by the facility, inquire about liability insurance and make sure you have enough to be covered in case of an injury or a problem with the facility. If you are an independent contractor, you will have to purchase your own liability insurance.

Equipment

Of course you will need an adequate sound system. If you are teaching at a recreation facility, nightclub, dance studio, or health club, chances are the house system is good, which means one less investment for you. But if you are in an unequipped gym or building or if you travel to teach on special occasions, you will have to consider bringing your own system.

The least expensive option is a portable sound system consisting of a CD (compact disc) player and two small speakers that are combined in one unit—the type you can buy at your local department or audio store. This is fine for a small group in an indoor area, and it is also inexpensive and easy to cart around. The disadvantage is that this type of system often does not provide enough volume for large groups, and you cannot attach a microphone to it.

The next higher grade of sound system is a more expensive self-contained unit that includes a CD player and/or cassette deck with speed-control. The speed-control feature is extremely beneficial when instructing beginning students. This system also includes a microphone, amplifier, and two speakers. It has separate volume controls for the microphone and music. This sound system, which is similar to a karaoke machine, is great for instructing groups of 50 to 80 because it is louder and clearer than the previous system. The entire system can be enclosed in a portable case with handles. It can be purchased at music equipment stores that cater to musicians and disc jockeys. The disadvantages are that most systems of this type do not work with cordless microphones and their volume is limited. In addition, the speakers on these systems face only one direction so there are limitations on being able to hear them, and the microphone may create interference if used by someone standing in front of the speakers.

The best equipment is a professional sound system similar to that used by disc jockeys. This type of system should not be confused with a home sound system. The most important benefits of using a professional system are the sound quality and volume. A professional system is also much more durable and can provide greater amplification without damaging the speakers. A complete professional sound system includes an amplifier, CD and/or cassette player, mixing board, cordless microphone, two speakers, and/or a case. The mixing board adjusts the volume of the microphone in relation to the music and can give you the freedom of playing music continuously from your CD player or your cassette deck—just like a disc jockey. The CD player or cassette deck with speed-control creates a wonderful method of teaching. Two-hundred fifty to 300 watts per speaker is a good standard of volume to use when instructing a large group in a building such as a gymnasium.

This type of system gives you complete control over the volume of your voice in relation to your music. It can cater to the following types of higher quality microphone:

- Wireless (no cord on the microphone and it is held in the hand)
- Lapel (no cord is attached to the microphone and it is attached to the clothing near your face)
- Headset (no cord is attached to the microphone and it goes over your ears so the microphone is right by your mouth)

Headset microphones provide for the best mobility, so that you can move your head while talking or walk anywhere in the building without interference or fluctuation in the voice. To properly speak into a microphone, the head of the microphone should be at the center of the chin. Even on a headset model, the microphone should be at the center of the chin for the best reception. Too much volume on the microphone setting compared to the master volume control can cause feedback from the speakers. Also, you do not want to stand directly in front of the speakers.

You can purchase speakers separately to accommodate the volume needed for your facility and the size of your group, but they must be compatible with your amplifier. A CD player that comes with a remote control can be an advantage. If you are helping students on the dance floor and you do not have the time to run back to the sound system to change the music, just press the remote! All these units can be purchased individually to satisfy your needs, and most come with a three-year warranty. Prices vary depending on the quality you desire. Except for the speakers, the system can fit into a rack mountable case for easy storage and mobility. Don't forget long speaker cables! Of course. you will need a bigger budget for this type of sound system, but it will be well worth it as the system can last for years if maintained properly.

Music

And now for the music. What music do you play? What if students do not like your music? Relax. Just like a disc jockey, you must play a variety. Watch how your students react to the songs. Be assertive, but do not stray away from the popular songs. Maybe you have heard a particular song over and over again, but your students have not. Be open! Remember, you are there for your students. For variety, try changing the music. Practice the line dances to funk, disco, techno, Latin, and Big Band.

If you are still using some phonograph records, be aware that they will be harder to purchase in the future. CDs are your best bet. They have an advantage over cassettes not only because of their sound quality, but also because you do not have to waste time rewinding and fast-forwarding. Waiting for an instructor to fiddle with music affects the flow of the class and the motivation of the students.

What songs should you use? Well, first you can use the music suggested in this book, which was put together based on a national survey. Or you can check out the latest charts in your local music store or on the Internet for the listing of the 10 top sellers. Listen to the songs first and check the BPMs before purchasing. See if the rhythms complement the dances. A local disc jockey may be able to give you more advice. Although buying the latest music is an advantage in teaching, it can be expensive. Talk to the manager at your local music store and ask for an instructor's discount if you refer your students' business to the store. Another idea is to have students bring in music they enjoy. However, always review this music for bad lyrics and proper BPMs before playing it in class. If your time is limited, you may consider joining a mail-order or Internet music club. But be aware that these clubs may require contracts and that their prices are sometimes higher than in your local music store.

If you are self-employed, you must obtain licenses to use the music you choose from the American Society of Composers, Authors and Publishers (ASCAP) and Broadcast Music, Inc. (BMI).

Attire

Your clothing should be clean and appropriate for the setting. Dress like a professional. Your personal attire creates an atmosphere and motivates your students. Attending line dance class is similar to a social event, so dress in the proper attire for your environment. Today, almost anything goes. Check out the yellow pages for fashion ideas or visit the Internet. (If you are planning on wearing a wireless microphone, make sure you have a belt or pant or pocket to attach the transmitter.)

For footwear, boots or comfortable walking shoes are the best; but almost any type of footwear can do except for shoes with rubber soles, shoes with very high heels, and sandals. (Just think of the liability problem you may have if someone's sandals fly off and hit someone else while you are teaching a kick!) Of course, socks and bare feet are not suitable. In health clubs, the main focus is physical fitness, so the appropriate attire for this environment is loose-fitting clothing or sweats with aerobic shoes. Cross-training shoes are actually best for fitness.

Students wearing athletic shoes should use caution when doing turns and should be sure to pick up their feet to avoid ankle problems. They should also avoid very high heels due to the strain on the lower back. If the floor is slippery, students should wear suede-bottom shoes or a very thin rubber backing on the soles of their shoes.

Class Format

Now that you're sounding and looking good, let's talk about class format. The most successful formula for teaching class is to offer a four to six week course that meets once a week for one to two hours. This arrangement will neither discourage the beginners nor bore the more experienced students. When you begin your next session, do not be discouraged if students do not return; turnover is expected. There are many reasons why students may not want to continue, ranging from not having enough personal time to feeling that they have enough material to keep them happy for awhile. As you begin the new line dance session, offer two courses: beginning- and intermediate-level. At the end of this session, offer another series of beginning and intermediate courses and also add an advanced-level class. After observing class enrollment, you will have to determine whether you should keep channeling students into the advanced class or create new classes, perhaps ones that combine the intermediate and advanced levels. Whatever way you decide to go, you should offer variety in the classes, such as the opportunity to work on style, perform in groups, or prepare for dance competitions.

Let's pretend this is your first day of class and you have butterflies in your stomach. What is the very first thing you should do? Relax and talk to your students. Be yourself. Students love honesty. Then begin your lesson with a class format such as the following (although you may need to adjust the time to fit your designated teaching time slot):

1. *Welcome the class.* Give them a general orientation on what to expect. This will help them prepare mentally and emotionally. Give the students a chance to get to know each other by having them shake hands or by telling you the name of their favorite song. Always encourage verbal sharing of ideas.

2. *Put on some popular music and get moving.* Here's a secret about teaching—keep the music going, even lightly in the background, when you are teaching and keep your students active. If this is an intermediate class, review some previously learned line dances. If it's a beginning class, have the students practice walking patterns, such as a grapevine to the right and left or walking to the rhythm forward and back. Try teaching some of the steps by half-counting—stepping on every other beat first and repeating the steps up to tempo—to familiarize the students with steps they are going to encounter. If this is the second or third class, review any dances already learned.

3. *Present a new line dance—always start with a beginning dance.* Teach the new dance step by step and build on each progression. Keep repeating the name of the step as you teach it. Teach the dance at a slow tempo and repeat, repeat, repeat! Begin by always facing one wall, even if the dance is a two- or four-wall dance, until the students are proficient. If you do not have mirrors, demonstrate the dances with your back to the students. Then try facing your students, but remember that you will have to dance in the same direction as the students, which means you will need to learn the dance in opposition! This may be a challenge at first, but after practicing a while it will come easily. And your smiling face, while they are dancing, will be appreciated.

When you feel the students are ready, walk through the dance facing the different specified directions (or walls) before doing it to music. Try to have a leader in the front of the group so when they change directions they have someone to follow. Only teach a few phrases at a time and repeat to make sure most students understand before you continue. Nothing is more frustrating for a student than to be taught too much at one time. A good exercise is to have students close their eyes as you call out the steps slowly. Another exercise is to have students count the beats out loud as they practice. If you have a student who is having trouble keeping up with the rhythm, keep encouraging him or her to practice, and perhaps offer half-hour private lessons before or after class.

4. *Try "cueing" before the dancers perform the steps.* Vocal cues are the short-step descriptions or directions you give the dancers to remind them what step is coming up next. Just one word or phrase, a few counts before the steps are performed, cues the dancers for the next move and gives them a chance to perform the steps without stopping to guess what comes next. Once the students have accomplished the steps, try counting the beats for them. Most instructors start line dances by counting out loud

"5-6-7-8." This alerts the dancers to begin on the "1" count. To help you get the feel, count to yourself "1-2-3-4" and then say "5-6-7-8" out loud to the beat of the music. This insures your call is in tempo or rhythm, which really helps the dancers get off to a good start. Then turn up the music and watch them dance!

5. *Try the new dance to different songs and tempos.* This will keep the class interested and motivated. Let the students talk after they have learned a sequence. It will give them the opportunity to relax and release tension. Encouraging a social atmosphere is another one of the objectives of dance.

6. *Schedule a break to discuss details, review the entire dance slowly, give pointers, and work on style.* During the break time, encourage dancers to drink water. It will keep up their energy level. You can also use this time to answer questions, show video clips, or talk about style or technique. You may want to discuss retail outlets for music and attire or mention places to go dancing. And you could even bring in a guest to teach or perform.

7. *Repeat complete dances again until the class is proficient (which means the majority have it).* Then review any previously learned dances, one after the other, making sure the majority have successfully completed each dance before going on to the next one. Always keep the music going! This will give the students a sense of accomplishment as well as motivate them to keep dancing.

8. *Allow five minutes at the end of class for questions or individual attention and "bonding."* This is a great time for teachers because it is when they get their best feedback and have a chance to get to know class participants personally. And be sure to give the students something to look forward to by telling them a little bit about your next lesson.

9. *Make notes about what you taught and jot down ideas for the next class.* The best time to prepare for your next lesson is when everything is still fresh in your mind.

10. *Use a different format if you are teaching line dance aerobics.* The purpose of aerobic line dancing is to exercise the body, especially the heart. You should know how to take target heart rates. Being certified is very important. Remember to keep the dances simple and repeat segments of them as necessary. Be sure to adjust the BPMs of the songs you are using to the class fitness level. The following format is based on a 40 to 60 minute class. Adjust the time to fit your class as necessary.

5-10 minutes	Get the body temperature up by doing walking patterns. If this is not your first class, review previously learned line dances.
3-5 minutes	Stretch the appropriate muscle groups, making sure the calves, hamstrings, and hip area are warmed up sufficiently.
20-30 minutes	Perform continuous line dance patterns facing one wall until the class is proficient enough to face other walls. It is important to keep the class moving. Implement marches in place as you "add on" the line dance movements in proper progression. The marches allow students to relax mentally and prepare for the next dance step. Add arm and upper body movements to expand the workout. Be sure to decrease the beats per minute during the last 5 minutes (cooldown).
10-15 minutes	If time permits, include conditioning for the abdominal muscles and upper torso area.
5 minutes	Cool down with slow stretching movements.

Teaching in the Schools

Teaching dance in the public schools is different, as you are working with students who are required to come to your class. This creates a challenging situation in teaching since you probably will be working with higher numbers of students and your class time lengths may vary. Consider teaching a two-week unit to grades K through 3, a three-week unit to grades 4 through 6, a five-week unit to grades 7 and 8, and a six-week unit or longer to grades 9 and above. Don't be concerned about students who are better dancers than you are. Just teach the steps and let them put their own style into it. Use the high-ability dancers as leaders for the class. This will keep the advanced students motivated and enhance their self-esteem. Encourage them to bring music to class that will motivate them. And remember that you will get better at teaching the dances as you gain experience.

Teaching every day and all day can wear on you and make you susceptible to injury. You must be aware of your body and pace yourself. For example, once the students learn a dance, have them perform for each other so as to give your body a rest. Bring in a video camera and have the students watch themselves for learning purposes. Another idea is to have the students create a dance on their own. One way to do this is to select eight dancers and have them each give you four counts of their favorite dance steps. Have the rest of the class learn the steps, as you add all of these individual steps together to form your own class choreography routine. Select some music and have the eight dancers call out their steps as you get to their moves.

Additional Suggestions

1. *Be prompt, organized, and ready to take control.* Most students attend class because of you, so having a regular substitute teacher is not a good idea if you want students to come back.

2. *Be positive in order to create an emotionally safe and enjoyable learning environment.* Have a sense of humor and be friendly, enthusiastic, and personable. Remember that most of your students take the class for recreational reasons, not to become professional dancers. Make it easy. If you can't do it, chances are they can't either. Avoid partner dances at first. Take a low-key approach to avoid self-consciousness.

3. *Be firm, yet compassionate.* Establish whatever rules are necessary to maintain control. Take responsibility for your authority, but be sensitive to the students' feelings.

4. *Know your students.* Learn their names and the types of music they enjoy. Be a good listener and learner. Make your students feel important. Be flexible. Your students will respect you if you keep up-to-date.

5. *Use good eye contact.* Do not favor individual students. Make corrections on a positive note, reinforcing what the student should do rather than what he or she should not do. Students should never be afraid to make mistakes.

6. *Give clear directions.* Keep your instructions light—not too technical. Try to cue before the movement. Call out the detailed steps first, then abbreviate the cues to the suggested words listed with each dance. Finally, call out the number of counts in the

line dance. Avoid carbonated soft drinks and alcohol, as they dehydrate you and hamper your speaking ability.

7. *Adapt to your students' ages and ability levels.* If you are teaching young children and they are having difficulty learning a routine, simplify it with an easier variation. But be sure the students know it is a variation, so they do not get discouraged when they show off their new line dance to their friends and find out it is not the real dance!

8. *Expand your teaching arena.* Teach at mixers and social functions. But be sure to know yourself and your limitations, and take care of yourself. Too much teaching can be hard on the body and may even burn you out mentally.

9. *Remember that attitude shows!* Don't ever compete or show you are better than your students. Remember, there will always be someone better and worse than you. You are there to help them achieve their goals. Enjoy what you do, and your students will too!

Dance education, continuing throughout life, benefits the body, mind, and spirit.

Life's a dance

You learn as you go

Sometimes you lead

Sometimes you follow

Don't worry about what you don't know

Life's a dance

You learn as you go.

—*John Michael Montgomery*

For information on other Christy Lane dance instructional products, visit her Web site at **www.christylane.com**, or call 800-555-0205.